connecting *to the*
power *of* nature

About the Author

Joe H. Slate, Ph.D. (Alabama), is a licensed psychologist and Emeritus Professor of Psychology at Athens State University. The U.S. Army and the Parapsychology Foundation of New York have funded his lab projects in parapsychology. His research led to the establishment of the Parapsychology Research Foundation. Dr. Slate has appeared on several radio and television shows, including *Strange Universe* and *Sightings*.

To Write to the Author

If you wish to contact the author or would like more information about this book, please write to the author in care of Llewellyn Worldwide and we will forward your request. Both the author and publisher appreciate hearing from you and learning of your enjoyment of this book and how it has helped you. Llewellyn Worldwide cannot guarantee that every letter written to the author can be answered, but all will be forwarded. Please write to:

Joe H. Slate Ph.D.
℅ Llewellyn Worldwide
2143 Wooddale Drive. 978-0-7387-1566-7
Woodbury, Minnesota 55125-2989, U.S.A.

Please enclose a self-addressed stamped envelope for reply, or $1.00 to cover costs. If outside U.S.A., enclose international postal reply coupon.

connecting *to the*
power *of* nature

JOE H. SLATE PH.D.

Llewellyn Publications
Woodbury, Minnesota

131

631

First Edition
First Printing, 2009

Book design by Donna Burch
Cover and interior art © DigitalVision
Cover design by Ellen Dahl
Editing by Connie Hill
Llewellyn is a registered trademark of Llewellyn Worldwide, Ltd.

Library of Congress Cataloging-in-Publication Data
Slate, Joe H.
  Connecting to the power of nature / Joe H. Slate. — 1st ed.
      p.   cm.
  Includes bibliographical references and index.
  ISBN 978-0-7387-1566-7
  1. Parapsychology. 2. Nature—Psychic aspects. I. Title.
  BF1040.S53   2009
  131—dc22   2009029346

Llewellyn Publications
A Division of Llewellyn Worldwide, Ltd.
2143 Wooddale Drive, Dept. 978-0-7387-1566-7
Woodbury, Minnesota 55125-2989, U.S.A.
www.llewellyn.com

Printed in the United States of America

I go to nature to be soothed and healed,
And to have my senses put in tune once more.
—JOHN BURROUGHS

Those who contemplate the beauty of the earth find reserves
of strength that will endure as long as life lasts.
—RACHEL CARSON

CONTENTS

Acknowledgements

I am deeply grateful to the many individuals—far more than I can name—who participated in the production of this book. I am especially grateful to the scores of college students whose critical suggestions broadened my perspective and sharpened much of my thinking. You are a part of this book, and I owe you far more than I can say.

To my academic colleagues, thank you for your encouragement, criticisms, and insightful contributions. You were always willing to share not only your specialized knowledge but your larger reflections and broader concerns. You gave far more than I could have anticipated.

I owe an enormous debt of gratitude to Debra Glass for her encouragement and invaluable suggestions for the duration of this project. Also to Marc A. Slate and Scott Morgan, I express my deepest appreciation. Thank you!

A special word of appreciation goes to the Parapsychology Research Foundation for its unflagging support of my work. Established at Athens State University in 1970, the Foundation, now an off-campus organization under the direction of Judge Sam Masdon, continues to promote the discovery of new knowledge through its educational, research, and endowment programs.

Though it may seem extreme to some of my readers, I must include in these acknowledgements my appreciation of the magnificent animal beings that have been invaluable sources of insight and inspiration throughout my life. They too are an important part of this book. Without animal beings, from the lowliest to the most advanced, this planet would be a lonely, austere place.

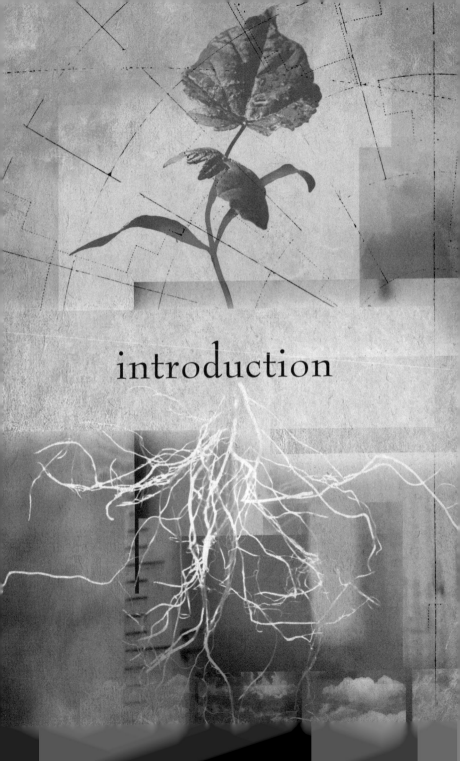

introduction

The heart of so great a mystery can never be reached
by following one road only.
—Q. AURELIUS SYMMACHUS

From a handful of sand to the most distant star, nature invites you to experience its hidden side. Through your interactions with nature, you will discover an exciting new gateway to self-empowerment. You will experience totally new powers, both within yourself and beyond. Enlightenment, inspiration, happiness, and success are all within your reach when you tap into the power of nature.

The step-by-step programs presented in this book are designed to awaken your dormant potentials and empower you to reach your highest goals through interacting with nature. You will discover effective ways of dissolving growth blockages, achieving career success, increasing creativity, enriching social relationships, resolving conflicts, breaking unwanted habits, managing stress, and solving personal problems. You will even learn how to slow the aging process and in some instances, actually reverse the signs of aging. The end result is an attuned, balanced, and empowered state of mind, body, and spirit that simply cannot fail.

Admittedly, we do not know all there is to know about the unseen side of nature, nor do we know all there is to know about our own existence. There is powerful evidence that existing within each of us is a vast storehouse of past experiences not presently available to conscious awareness. Add to that the enormous wealth of undeveloped potential existing in everyone, and the challenge to reach our highest destiny becomes even greater.

In view of that complex challenge, I've included in this book an extensive range of programs and methods, some of which embrace nontraditional approaches not yet fully integrated into conventional science. We know from the past that when the dots are finally connected, there's but a thin line between traditional and nontraditional orientations. As William James put it, "We have to live today by what truth we can get today, and be ready tomorrow to call it falsehood." The absence of conventional recognition alone should not prevent us from exploring nontraditional approaches and experiencing their effectiveness for ourselves.

Because firsthand experience provides the clearest and most convincing evidence of the empowerment relevance of nature, I've included in this book many of my personal experiences, some of them reaching into the early formative years of childhood. You'll also find in these pages scores of experiences reported by others, including my students and associates. Collectively, they illustrate an amazing range of possibilities available to everyone through interacting with nature.

You'll find at the back of this book a seven-day plan that further explores nature as a gateway to personal empowerment. Each day of the plan introduces an objective and a step-by-step program specifically formulated to achieve it. Through the plan, you will discover workable ways of enriching the quality of your life while contributing to a better world. All the resources you need are within your grasp—the plan empowers you to take hold of them.

Throughout this book, I've emphasized the critical importance of nurturing and protecting our natural environment. Our planet does not come with a backup or replacement plan. Although nature could conceivably turn on us at any moment with its wandering black holes, collapsing stars, and trekking asteroids, we alone are our gravest threat. Reckless exploitation of natural resources, destruction and degradation of animal habitats, and irresponsible pollution of the environment leave more than transient footprints—they inflict gaping wounds with potentially catastrophic consequences for both present and future generations. Now is the time to heal the Earth. Although what we've been in the past and what we'll be in the future are important, it's what we do *now* that's critical. Now is the time to work together to make the world a safer, better place for present and future generations. We must find ways on a massive scale to reduce deforestation, protect endangered and threatened species, and reverse global warming. It's my hope that this book will contribute to that important effort by bringing forth in each of us a greater appreciation of our shared planet and a lasting commitment to care for it.

In your application of this book's self-empowerment procedures that include the use of nature's indigenous flora as well as nonindigenous exotic species, one should be aware of those that pose the threat of allergies or the potential of toxins. This would include any plant part or derivatives, i.e., seeds, bark, leaves, flowers, sap, and so forth.

SUMMARY

Self-discovery and self-empowerment—they go hand in hand with each contributing to the other. Nature in its full splendor challenges you at this moment to discover for yourself its hidden side as a gateway to self-empowerment. In the pages that follow, you'll find exciting new ways of doing just that!

1: star power

Out yonder there was this huge world ... which stands before us like a great eternal riddle ...

—ALBERT EINSTEIN

As a young boy growing up in the country, viewing the night sky with its spectacular display of stars expanded my small world and connected me to the universe. But rather than being overwhelmed by the universe, I was both challenged and emboldened by it. The Milky Way stretching from sky to sky gave compelling evidence that "big things are just small things put together." At an early age, I became convinced that I could take small things and put them together to achieve any goal, regardless of size. Beyond the known universe, I reasoned, were others yet to be discovered, and I felt connected to all of them, as well as the vast energy space between them.

I also began early on to question the origin of my existence. I quickly became convinced that my existence was not limited to this physical reality. I somehow knew that I had come from another dimension, and that I would one day return to it. I embraced at an early age the concept of bi-directional endlessness of life, though I didn't know to call it that. If the soul exists forever after death, I reasoned, it logically existed forever before birth. You can't have one without the other, I concluded. I also concluded that the soul is not simply a thing I possess—if it were merely a possession, I could lose it, or even worse it could somehow be taken from me. The soul was for me the great *I Am,* the essential essence of my being. I came to believe that my destiny, along with that of all souls, is endless growth and immeasurable greatness. Even if I'm wrong, I thought, I'm richer for believing it. Till this day, those early concepts about the nature of my existence and that of all souls remain essentially unchanged.

When I looked at the stars as a child, a single star usually grabbed my attention. Though it wasn't always the brightest star, I at once felt somehow linked to it as a gateway to the cosmos at large. I knew that whatever force lay beyond the star existed also within my own being, as well as in the world around me. It was for me the collective force that energized and sustained all that exists, both seen and unseen. Only much later would I find a name for it—*the life force.*

It was also much later that, as a psychologist and college professor, I would develop numerous programs designed to promote empowering interactions with nature. Early among them was *Star Gaze.*

STAR GAZE

Star Gaze is a step-by-step program based on the simple premise that self-enlightenment is power. It embraces the concept that the greater your understanding of yourself and the meaning of your existence, the more empowered you become to actualize your potentials and achieve your highest goals.

Star Gaze uses a selected star as a point of focus to promote self-enlightenment and empowerment. It's an energizing approach that recognizes higher consciousness itself as a repository of power and a manifestation of ultimate reality. It acknowledges the divine nature of our being and our ability to directly experience it. It's often through Star Gaze that profound new insight unfolds with life-changing impact.

Aside from its enlightening and energizing effects, Star Gaze is a practical program that targets designated personal goals and empowers you to achieve them. All that's required is the night sky with its magnificent display of stars and a willingness to interact with them. When stars are unavailable for viewing, you can use an easy but effective adaptation of the program in which the starry sky is simply visualized.

Here's the program.

Step 1. Night Scan

Find a quiet, safe, relaxing place and view the night sky with its vast display of stars. Allow plenty of time to scan the full sky. Notice the various clusters of stars and the patterns they form. If stars are unavailable for viewing, you can close your eyes and use visualization to create a starry sky of your own.

Step 2. Star-glow Effect

Select a certain star and focus your full attention on it. Think of that star as your link to the collective life force underlying the universe and all that exists within and beyond it. With your attention centered on the star, slowly expand your peripheral vision to take in the vastness of space from horizon to horizon. As you hold that expanded view, let your eyes fall slightly out of focus and you will immediately notice a radiant glow enveloping first the star and then the full heavens, a phenomenon I call the *star-glow effect.* Sense the deep relaxation and peaceful state of mind that typically accompany this remarkable phenomenon.

Step 3. Solar Plexus Star

Close your eyes and shift your awareness to your solar plexus as the quiet center of your innermost self. Think of that bright center as your *solar plexus star.* Take plenty of time to experience that special place of inner quietness and peace.

Step 4. Peak Infusion

As your eyes remain closed, visualize the distant star with a bright beam of light connecting it to the solar plexus star within yourself. Sense the powerful infusion of energy surging throughout your total being to empower you mentally, physically, and spiritually. Once the surge of energy reaches its peak, embrace the deep sense of oneness with the universe that usually accompanies that moment. It's at this point that spiritual enlightenment to include awareness of a guiding spirit presence often emerges. Let yourself become aware of totally new possibilities in your life.

Step 5. Goal Statement

As you continue to experience your connection to the distant star, specify your goals, limiting them to no more than three. Visualize each goal as a future reality poised for fulfillment. Think of the star as a manifestation of your destiny for success.

Step 6. Conclusion

Conclude the program by bringing your hands together as a symbol of attunement and balance. With your hands joined, affirm in your own words your oneness with the highest realms of power.

After completing Star Gaze, you can at any time activate its empowering effects in an instant by simply bringing your hands together while visualizing a distant star with a beam of light connecting you to it. This inconspicuous cue called simply *Reinforcement Visualization* is especially important for long-term goals. It's also highly effective as a stress management technique. It can instantly generate inner balance while building feelings of adequacy and well-being.

Over the years, I've recommended Star Gaze to my students and clients alike. Insight of important therapeutic relevance often surfaces spontaneously during its use—at times with life-changing impact, as illustrated by a university administrator who used the program to overcome a lifelong fear of enclosed spaces. The fear, by her report, was so intense that it severely constricted her life, always hanging over her "like a dark, sinister cloud." During the energy surge in Step 4, she experienced an easy release of all fear. Today, she attributes her total freedom from fear of enclosed places to Star Gaze, which promptly extinguished it. She did for herself through Star Gaze what extensive psychotherapy had failed to accomplish. By her report, Star Gaze put her in touch with the best of all therapists—the one deep within herself.

As noted, awareness of a guiding presence often accompanies this program, particularly during the peak energy infusion in Step 4. Significant interactions with the spirit realm, however, can occur at any point in the program, as well as during Reinforcement Visualization that follows it. It was in fact during Reinforcement Visualization that a real estate broker experienced the profound awareness of a spirit presence accompanied by the distant sound of orchestral music. Inspired by the experience and her belief that music is the language of the universe, she went to work at once to establish in record time a symphony orchestra in her hometown. She credits in large measure the extraordinary success of the orchestra to the spirit guide she came to know through Star Gaze.

If you prefer, you can use the moon instead of the star as an effective point of focus for this program. The glow effect that accompanies this adaptation in Step 2 is called, as you might expect, the *moon-glow effect* which is often more pronounced than the star-glow effect, particularly when the moon is in its full phase. Except for the substitution of the moon for the star, the program remains unchanged.

STAR TRAVEL

Spontaneous impressions of being out of the physical body and traveling to a spatially distant location have been known to occur during Star Gaze, particularly in Step 4. Since the results of these impressions were typically profound, the program was modified to facilitate productive out-of-body travel and firsthand interaction with distant sources of power. The resultant program called *Star Travel* is based on the concept that the astral body as the physical body's non-biological double is endowed with the capacity to disengage the physical body, and while in that state, to travel in astral form to other dimensions and planes of power. Enlightenment, wellness, rejuvenation, and inspiration, to mention but a few of the possibilities, are all within the scope of Star Travel. Here's the program.

Step 1. Star View
Find a quiet, safe place free of distractions, and while resting in a comfortable, reclining position, view the night sky with its wide canvas of stars. Note the various arrangements of stars and their differences in color, size, and brightness. (As with Star Gaze, you can use mental imagery to visualize stars when a night sky is unavailable for viewing.)

Step 2. Visualization
Close your eyes and visualize the spacious display of stars. Note your sense of serenity and complete peace with the

universe as your mind becomes free of clutter and your physical body becomes increasingly relaxed.

Step 3. Projected Awareness

As your eyes remain closed, continue to visualize the wide display of stars stretching from sky to sky until a single star commands your attention. Sense your connection to that star as your link to the cosmos and your personal gateway to the highest realms of power. Allow images of that realm with its radiant astral planes of color to unfold as you mentally envelop your total being with bright, protective energy. Affirm, "I am enveloped and shielded with the bright energy of the highest realms of power."

Step 4. Astral Interaction

As the colorful planes unfold before you, note your sense of weightlessness and physical disengagement as you are drawn to them, not as an elusive dimension but as a present reality. Allow plenty of time for full astral engagement of that reality. One by one, embrace its various planes of color and bathe in each of them to infuse your total being with new power. You can at once become infused with healing and rejuvenating energy by interacting with planes of radiant green. You can experience peace, serenity, and a complete state of well-being by interacting with planes of blue. You can promote intellectual skills and accelerate learning by interacting with radiant planes of yellow. You can gain spiritual enlightenment by interacting with planes of indigo. It's during these interactions that awareness of spiritual teachers, ministering guides, and growth specialists often emerges as warm, nurturing companions. You will notice the complete absence of negative forces as you interact with the various planes of color.

Step 5. Disengagement and Return

Once your interactions are complete, let yourself disengage the astral realm by first shifting your attention to your physical body at rest at a distance while sensing your connection to it. Then give yourself permission to return to your physical body and re-engage it. Allow plenty of time for full re-engagement to occur. Let yourself become increasingly aware of your breathing and such physical sensations as warmth or coolness and body weight. Once re-engagement is complete, note the physical relaxation and peaceful state of mind.

Step 5. Reflection

As you remain relaxed, take time to reflect on the experience. Focus on its empowerment significance as new insight and awareness of totally new possibilities unfold. Sense your complete attunement to the universe.

Step 6. Conclusion

Conclude the experience with affirmations of personal well-being and success. Examples are: "I am at my peak mentally, physical, and spiritually. All the resources I need are now available to me. I am fully empowered to achieve my highest goals."

Upon completing this program, notice any lingering impressions of the astral realm. Remind yourself that the astral dimension is a potentially empowering reality of vital importance to your life. Let yourself remain attuned to it and infused with its energies. This simple exercise can become a profound peak experience.

SUMMARY

As you explore the empowering side of nature, it's reassuring to know that the universe and the powers that sustain it are constantly receptive to your probes and interactions. Through Star Gaze and Star Travel, you can experience new sources of power along with the very essence of your being as an endless soul. By reaching for the stars (or the moon) and interacting with them, you can become attuned to the universe at large, as well as the innermost part of your being. With the limitless powers of the universe at your command, you can achieve your loftiest goals and fully experience the inner life force that is the essential you. Who could ask for more than that?

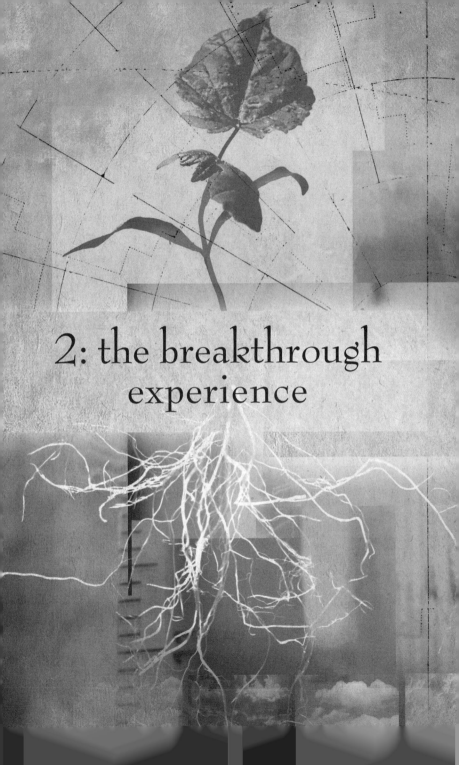

2: the breakthrough experience

The meaning of life is arrived at ... by dark gropings,
by feelings not fully understood, by catching for hints
and fumbling for explanations.

—Alfred Adler

Do you remember the moment you first realized you were at the brink of a major breakthrough? For me, it happened as a young boy when I unexpectedly experienced a life-changing encounter with nature's hidden side.

Growing up in the country, I often explored a nearby forest with my best friend who lived within bicycling range. Each of our excursions into the magnificent forest untouched by axe or saw increased our appreciation of its wondrous sights and sounds—rushing streams, great rock formations, bird calls from its shadowy depths, and a distant waterfall with an enormous cave hidden behind it.

But nothing about the deep forest interested us more than its gigantic trees, some interlaced with branches so dense that only faint specks of sky could be seen through them. We occasionally camped overnight under a certain rugged oak where we speculated that Native Americans had also camped, as suggested by the many arrowheads and other artifacts we found in the area. We once looped a rope over a lower limb to fashion a makeshift swing, and imagined that an outlaw in olden days could have been hanged at sunset from that same limb.

With my friend looking on, I once climbed the magnificent tree. Upon reaching its uppermost branches, I somehow lost my grip and crashed to the ground where my head struck a gnarled root that crawled out, dragon-like, from the tree's massive trunk. In a state I can describe only as shadowy, I felt myself ascending effortlessly, first winding slowly through the tree's dense foliage and then rising rapidly above the forest until it became a small patch of emerald green surrounded by sun-filled meadows studded with silver lakes. It was my first aerial view of Earth in all its startling, untouched beauty.

As I remained suspended in space far above that magnificent scene, a brilliant transparent sphere from out of the blue quietly formed around me. Safely crouched within the iridescent orb, I saw looming on a distant horizon a spectacular display of bright planes, all equally spaced one above the other like richly colored layers of cirrus clouds at sunset. I somehow knew there was more to the amazing scene than what met the eye. Suddenly, radiant beams shot forth from the distant planes like stunning fireworks, targeting the sphere and bathing it with multicolored brilliance.

As the bright beams continued to shower the sphere, I experienced a powerful infusion of energy unlike anything I'd ever known before. It was a self-defining moment! I felt instantly linked to the universe, totally attuned to it and it with me. The sphere, unlike a restrictive vehicle, had broken all barriers. It was a liberating force that engaged a totally new dimension of reality. It was a breakthrough experience I would always remember.

Once the cosmic fireworks ceased, the "sphere craft", as I called it, began a slow, spiraling descent, eventually circling the giant oak and finally coming to rest in the trembling shadows at the tree's base before dissolving away. I opened my eyes to see my friend bending over me, calling out to me by name. He helped me to my feet and checked me over for injury. Incredibly, except for a few minor scrapes, I was un-harmed. The tree's dense foliage and network of branches had braked the fall and granted a safe landing.

In ceremonious recognition, we placed our hands upon the tree's huge trunk and thanked it for its generous pro-tection. We then personalized the tree by naming it Gar-gon, after Gargon the Great, an early fictional hero of mine, and we marched around it like conquering warriors, boldly chanting its newly assigned name.

Following that incredible experience with Gargon, I al-ways thought of myself as a "tree person." I learned to in-teract with trees as not only earth's largest living things but towering antennae to the universe as well.

Although my experience with Gargon and the sphere craft was pivotal in my life at that early age, I didn't know exactly how to explain it. That night, before falling asleep, I wondered whether I had traveled outside my physical body, or was the experience simply a figment of my imagination? Could my escape from physical injury be the result of spiritual intervention, perhaps that of a spirit guardian, or was it simply a stroke of good luck? I wondered whether the experience gave proof of another dimension with many different planes of energy; or was it simply a product of temporary unconsciousness? While I tried not to read too much into the experience, I concluded at that early age that I had discovered firsthand a mysterious and marvelous gateway to a new dimension of amazing power. Little did I know then that I would devote much of my adult life as a psychologist to the study of that power.

I'll always remember another splendid tree in the old-growth forest, an aged beech I called Phoenix. At the tree's base was an everlasting spring known as Rock Fountain that flowed forcefully from the crevice of a large limestone boulder embraced by the roots of the enormous tree. Even during summer droughts, the unfailing spring sent forth a surging stream of cool, crystal clear water.

A few feet from the spring and overlooking it was a massive slab of limestone called Flat Rock. It was the perfect place for overnight camping. A tent set up on the rock in the shadow of Phoenix seemed always to amplify the whisper of trees and the mixed sounds of the everlasting fountain with its stream leaping over slippery green rocks and tumbling forth into placid pools. From a distance, the call of night creatures and the constant drumming of a waterfall reverberated throughout the primal forest as ghostly music composed by nature.

As a youngster, I often placed my hands upon Phoenix's silvery trunk to experience not only a connection to the tree but what seemed to be an infusion of its powerful energies. Time and again, my interactions with Phoenix seemed to generate healing energy, not only for myself but animal companions as well, including my injured dog of mixed breed named Zero. I had ridden horseback into the forest along a trail near Phoenix when the horse kicked Zero who was following too closely behind. I rushed the wailing dog to Phoenix and carefully placed him at the base of the tree. Suddenly I heard a rustling of Phoenix's leaves, though there was no breeze, whereupon Zero stopped wailing, stretched, and began leaping about with no sign of pain or injury, but cautiously keeping a safe distance from the horse. Inspired by Zero's amazing recovery, I brought other animals to Phoenix for healing. Never once disappointed, I became so connected to the great tree that I carved my initials into its massive trunk.

Over the years, I occasionally returned to the primal forest of my youth, with each visit awakening rich memories of my childhood experiences with it. But in a recent dream during which I viewed the forest from above, a dense gray haze completely concealed it. From my overhead view, I searched in vain for Phoenix, the oldest and tallest tree in the forest. Gargon, the magnificent oak that had protected me as a child when I fell from its heights, was likewise nowhere to be found.

Troubled by the vivid dream that seemed more like an out-of-body experience than a dream, I decided to visit the forest. From a distance, I saw as in my dream a dull gray cloud hanging over it. The cloud became even more ominous as I neared the forest. When I finally reached the site, I was unprepared for what I found. The great old-growth trees had been recently harvested, their remains piled like discarded bones in great heaps and set ablaze. Ashen columns of smoke rose from the still-smoldering heaps to support a vast, pallid canopy that stretched for miles shutting out the sunlight. The desiccated wasteland with its pungent odor showed no signs of life. Gargon had been torn from the earth, leaving behind a deep, open wound. Phoenix likewise had been recklessly ripped from the earth, dislodging the great boulder at its base and totally extinguishing the everlasting spring. Only Flat Rock remained unscathed. Though I'm not prone to tears, I wept as I surveyed the devastation.

Summary

Although Gargon and Phoenix no longer exist in objective reality, they remain forever etched in my mind. Together, they provided the master key that unlocked the hidden side of nature with its abundant growth resources. At an early age, I learned through them the value of those breakthrough experiences with nature that inspire, enlighten, and empower.

3: the power of trees

The passion for truth is silenced by answers which have the weight of undisputed authority.
—PAUL TILLICH

As magnificent antennae to the universe, trees are steadfast manifestations of nature's power and beauty. They can be spontaneously empowering by their sheer presence as earlier shown by the oak named Gargon and the beech named Phoenix. That said, could structured programs be designed to purposely access even greater power and directly target it toward designated goals? Fortunately, programs are now available to do just that. Inspiration, attunement, healing, rejuvenation, and enlightenment—to list but a few of the possibilities—are all within the scope of our interactions with trees.

Tree Power

Of all of the resources of nature, none is more receptive to our interactions than the tree. Merely beholding a splendid tree from a distance can be empowering, but experiencing it close up and actually touching it can be even more powerful. *Tree Power* is a self-empowerment program based on that simple premise. The easily administered five-step program requires first formulating a personal goal and then selecting a tree that seems relevant to your goal. In that context, the tree becomes a growth facilitator and valued gateway to success rather than simply a tangible object of nature. Here's the program.

Step 1. Identify Your Goal

Formulate your goal and visualize it as not merely a possibility but rather a future reality poised for fulfillment. Affirm in your own words your resolve to achieve your goal. Ironically, the simplest affirmation is typically the most powerful. The straightforward assertion, "I will achieve this goal," can set the stage for complete success.

Step 2. Select a Tree

Select a tree that appeals to you personally and seems appropriate to your stated goal.

Step 3. Engage the Tree

Engage the tree by first placing your hands near the tree's trunk, but without touching it. Upon again stating your goal as in Step 1, further engage the tree by resting your hands upon its trunk. (Note: You may choose at this point to give the tree a name using *free association*, by simply say-ing "tree" and allowing a name to come forth. Using free association to name the tree can activate a subconscious process that enriches your interaction with the tree.)

Step 4. Visualization and Affirmation

With your hands resting upon the tree, think of the tree as your link to the powers of nature. Again visualize your stated goal and affirm your success in achieving it. For instance, if your goal is health-related, picture yourself enveloped in a healthful glow and affirm, "I am fully infused with the en-ergies of health and fitness." If your goal is rejuvenation, vi-sualize yourself at your youthful prime and affirm, "This is the true me." If your goal is career success, visualize yourself established in the career of your choice and affirm, "I am destined for career success." Take your visualization a step further, if possible, by incorporating the tree into your goal-related imagery. For instance, if your goal is to overcome a persistent fear, imagine a bird taking flight from the tree, car-rying with it the fear and all the symptoms that accompa-nied it. As the bird soars into the distance, sense the release of fear and a fresh infusion of power replacing it. If your goal is health- and fitness-related, envision bright light as health-ful energy flowing from the tree into your hands and from there throughout your total body, bathing every organ and function until you are fully infused with radiant energy. To conclude this step, think of the tree as embracing your goal and transforming it into bright energy that goes forth into the universe to work in your behalf.

Step 5. Conclusion

Conclude the program by simply clasping your hands, a gesture that acknowledges the tree as a valued source of power. To reactivate at will the full effects of the procedure, you can use the handclasp gesture as a post-procedure cue, or you can return to the tree and simply place your hands upon it while visualizing your goal and affirming your success in achieving it.

As noted in Step 3, you may choose to name the tree using free association. Once you've named the tree, you can calculate the name's numerological significance by using a number/alphabet key that assigns a numerical value to each letter of the alphabet. (The Appendix provides detailed instructions for determining the numerological significance of names and dates.)

While various traditions regarding the empowerment relevance of specific trees differ widely, both the oak and beech are usually considered all-purpose trees and thus appropriate for almost any goal. They are, however, especially valued for goals related to health and prosperity. Here are a few examples of other trees and the empowerment relevance commonly assigned to them.

Maple and ash—creativity, intelligence, and intuitive insight.
Elm—tolerance, compassion, and understanding.
Hackberry—motivation and persistence.
Pine—vitality and instant infusion of energy.
Cedar—endurance and protection.

Poplar—enrichment, attunement, and balance.
Walnut and hickory—physical strength and wellness.
Magnolia—resilience and adaptation.
Sweet gum—rejuvenation, longevity, and healing.
Ginkgo—enlightenment, spirituality, and attunement.

It's important again to note that the assigned relevance of trees can vary widely among traditions. Selecting a tree that appeals to you personally and seems appropriate for your stated goal can be of far greater importance than traditional views that could constrict the tree's usefulness as an empowerment resource. Fortunately, the empowering relevance of trees remains unchanged, regardless of the season.

Strange though it may at first seem, the effectiveness of Tree Power as a self-empowerment program tends to increase with the introduction of color imagery. Trees seem to be receptive to color as suggested by the seasonal turning of their leaves along with the colorful blooms and fruits that characterize many of them. Further suggesting the affinity of trees for color is the common practice of tying ribbons of color around their trunks to commemorate an event or promote a cause.

Simply allowing imagery of a particular color to spontaneously unfold as you interact with the tree, particularly in Step 4, can be the best guide for your use of color in this program. Perhaps not unexpectedly, the emergent color imagery tends to be generally consistent with the significance of the various colors found in the human aura, the energy field enveloping the physical body. Here are a few examples of aura colors and their typically assigned relevance.

Light blue—tranquility, balance, and optimism.
Dark blue—mental alertness, emotional control, and
    endurance.
Pink—sensitivity, humanitarian concerns, and nurturing.
Yellow—intelligence, social interests, and problem solving.
Green—healing, rejuvenation, and self-actualization.
Orange—tenacity, assertiveness, and achievement.
Indigo—protection, enlightenment, and creativity.

Several of my students reported that wearing a clothing article of a relevant color, such as a headband or scarf, facilitated their use of color imagery and, in their opinion, improved the effectiveness of this program.

Promoting rejuvenation and wellness is one of the most popular and effective applications of Tree Power. For that goal, repetitive interactions with trees characterized by glossy, deep-green leaves, such as the sweet gum, is recommended. Although relevant imagery is important for all applications of this program, it's especially recommended for rejuvenation and health-related goals. During your interaction with the tree, visualizing yourself at your youthful prime enveloped in a radiant green glow can help jump-start the rejuvenation process and enrich the infusion of healthful energy. The dramatic effects of this program when practiced regularly will speak for themselves.

Along a different line, when practiced in the athletic setting, Tree Power has been especially effective for performance-related goals. In competitive sports, it can produce a profound energy surge that lasts for hours. When practiced individually or by a team immediately before a sports event, it can fire up determination and generate a decisive winning edge. For body building and developing complex athletic skills, regular practice of the program can increase the physical body's receptivity to training. Among my former students who practiced this program is an avid golfer who's convinced that regular practice of the Tree Power program significantly improved her game. Another student, a soccer player, claims that his use of the program dramatically improved his performance. Accomplished athletes typically prefer a large, stalwart tree combined with imagery of orange.

When applied in the academic setting, Tree Power has shown unusual effectiveness in building motivation and increasing self-confidence, both of which are conducive to academic success. With regular practice, the program when combined with imagery of yellow tends to boost overall mental efficiency to result in an increase in the rate of learning along with better recall, especially when used immediately before testing. Equally as important, students who routinely use the program report a marked increase in the simple pleasure of learning.

THE POWER OF HERCULES

At Athens State University, where I headed the psychology program for several years, stands one of the oldest and largest tulip trees in Alabama. Situated prominently in front of historic Founders Hall, the magnificent tree suggests an unusual abundance of powerful energy. According to legend, it was under the tree during the Civil War that the school's president, Jane Hamilton Childs, handed the commander of invading Federal troops a letter from President Lincoln that saved Founders Hall from destruction.

Given the history and prominence of the stalwart tree, it not surprisingly commanded the special interest students, including athletes who used it with the Tree Power Program to build their athletic skills. They together named the tree Hercules, in recognition of its value as an empowerment resource. As it turns out, the name Hercules has a single-digit numerical value of one which signifies independence and self-reliance, traits that seem particularly appropriate for this tree.

Hercules' influence as a natural resource reached far beyond athletics to include academic- and career-related goals. Over the years, many students routinely engaged Hercules as a valued academic resource. By their own reports, interacting with Hercules using the Tree Power Program prior to course examinations markedly improved their performance, particularly on tests requiring problem solving and analytical thinking. Along another line, Hercules gained considerable recognition among graduating seniors as a valued resource in their pursuit of career goals, including graduate study and job positions.

While Hercules can be seen as but another object of nature, almost everyone who interacts with the tree develops a strong connection to it. One of my former students, upon completing her doctorate in physics at a midwestern university, returned to campus to personally express her gratitude to Hercules for the academic inspiration it provided over the years, a function she called "distance enrichment." Hercules was for her "an academic icon." Another college student, a pre-law major, found through Hercules a complete liberation from the deep feelings of inferiority he attributed to early childhood abuse. In his words, "My interactions with Hercules banished all feelings of inferiority and replaced them with a strong sense of adequacy and worth."

Even goals related to romance do not appear to be beyond the scope of Hercules' influence as illustrated by an alumnus of the university who returned to campus for the school's annual Parapsychology Foundation Ball. As dusk descended on the evening of the ball, he used the Tree Power Program to engage Hercules in his search for true love. Almost instantly upon placing his hands against the tree, a clear mental image of a beautiful woman in red, wearing unusual scissors earrings, flashed before him as if brilliantly projected on a screen. Although skeptical of the significance of the image, that evening at the ball he met a strikingly beautiful fashion designer in red, wearing scissors earrings! His interaction with Hercules, he's convinced, prepared him for what he called a "magical moment."

Given these amazing examples, I was not surprised at the numerous accounts of Hercules' therapeutic relevance. Among the most striking instances is the testimony of a biology major who consulted Hercules in his effort to overcome a lifelong fear of spiders. Even pictures of spiders evoked such severe anxiety that he was considering changing his major. Conventional psychotherapy, including various cognitive-behavioral strategies, had utterly failed to extinguish his fear.

Upon approaching Hercules, he was fearful even from a distance that spiders, poised for an attack, were lurking somewhere in the tree's rugged trunk. But when he placed his hands with trembling anxiety against the tree, he felt an instant surge of energy so powerful that it banished all fear of spiders. Even the most ominous of spiders paled in comparison to the power of the magnificent tree. With his hands resting upon the tree and his eyes closed, the words **POWER AND FEAR CANNOT COEXIST** in bold, block letters flashed into his mind. By his own report, the experience with Hercules activated his subconscious powers and permanently extinguished all fear of spiders. Other students with other fears reported similar success.

Along a totally different line, I've personally interacted with Hercules for a variety of academic-related goals, including acquiring research grants and establishing student scholarships. When I, together with members of the Parapsychology Research Foundation, engaged the tree in an effort to secure research funding for a proposed study of altered states of consciousness, the Parapsychology Foundation of New York awarded a contract within days. The technical report for that study is available for inspection at the university's Library Archives (Slate, 1985). More recently, Hercules provided the seminal inspiration for establishing in perpetuity two student scholarships that are awarded annually—one at Athens State University and the other at the University of Alabama (Tuscaloosa).

Though it may seem highly speculative if not specious to some, Hercules has demonstrated over many years unusual receptivity to quartz crystals that have been programmed and then buried at the tree's base, a strategy we'll explore at depth in a later chapter. I've concluded that Hercules' powers as a giant antenna are unmatched when augmented by crystals with programmed energies that are consistent with those of the tree. At present, there is buried at Hercules' base a crystal specially programmed to promote the Parapsychology Research Foundation's goal of establishing a comprehensive research and development center.

Even after being struck by lightning, the regal tree, believed by some to be one of the oldest in Alabama, quickly recovered. With the closing of the deep gash along its trunk, it seemed to become even stronger than before. I've yet to uncover the limits of this great tree's powers.

MOVING AHEAD

As an undergraduate student at the University of Alabama, I was introduced by my fraternity to a group meditation program using circular seating around an aged magnolia on the grounds behind the fraternity house. The program, which became known as the Dr. M. Method, consisted simply of clearing the mind, slowing breathing, and progressively relaxing the body from the head region downward. Regularly meditating under the tree was thought by many students to literally increase their rate of learning and improve their retention of materials learned.

Years later, the Dr. M. Method would take on new life at Athens State University when a revised version called *Moving Ahead* was introduced as a major component in a remedial program for certain entering freshmen. In addition to their class work and tutoring, students enrolled in the remedial program participated regularly in Moving Ahead sessions conducted on campus in the shade of a large oak tree. Incredibly, all students upon successfully completing the remedial program rated Moving Ahead as its most important component. Here are the essential steps of the program which can be used individually or in groups with any tree of your choice.

Step 1. Tree Selection

Find a tree that appeals to you personally. Notice the tree's unique characteristics, including size, shape, and colors. Think of the tree as your connection to the power of nature.

Step 2. Relaxation

Settle back under the tree and with your eyes closed, take in a few deep breaths, taking a little longer to exhale. Let your mind become increasingly passive by initiating no active thought. As you breathe rhythmically, let relaxation spread throughout your body, beginning at your forehead and slowly progressing downward to the tips of your toes.

Step 3. Mental Imagery

Select a peaceful nature scene and focus your full attention on it. Examples include a tranquil moonlit lake, a walk in a park, a colorful sunset, or a cloud drifting in a breeze.

Step 4. Affirmation

Affirm in your own words your sense of personal empowerment and your destiny for success. Here are some examples: *I am at peace with myself and the universe. I am empowered to achieve my highest goals. Nothing can stop me now. Success is my destiny.* At this step, you may wish to specify a particular goal.

Step 5. Post-procedure Cue

Take a few moments to reflect on your affirmations and allow each of them to become an essential part of your innermost being. Conclude with the post-procedure cue that you can at any moment reactivate the program's full empowering effects as needed by a simple gesture of your choice, such as joining the tips of your fingers, stroking your ear lobe, or lifting a toe.

Formulated for use with any tree of choice, this step-by-step program can generate an attuned, balanced state that promotes achievement of almost any personal goal.

Although the Moving Ahead Program has nearly unlimited application, it's valued especially for self-development. The program has been unusually effective when used in the academic setting. While students are often amused when first introduced to Moving Ahead, they are usually quick to develop a strong respect for it. They, for the most part, find that interacting with a designated tree motivates them to meet even their most difficult academic challenges. As with Tree Power, students who use this program prior to course evaluations typically report a boost in brainpower and dramatic improvements in their test performance. When you're stressed out, it's an excellent way to generate a state of mental, physical, and spiritual attunement and balance.

This program has shown special effectiveness toward such goals as improving social relationships, achieving career success, losing weight, reducing stress, resolving conflict, and breaking unwanted habits, to list but a few. The program has been particularly effective when used to break the smoking habit. As with other quit-smoking approaches, Moving Ahead works best for instant quitting rather than tapering down. While simply stating a personal goal can build a strong resolve to achieve it, this program can give you the added resources required for your complete success.

With this program, any tree of choice can become a place of relaxation and introspection that clears your mind and connects you to a place of quietness within yourself. With its leaves catching a breeze, the tree, as one student put it, can *soothe the soul.* It can put you in touch with the best of all therapists—the one deep within yourself.

Though it may seem incredible at first, there are reports of trees that caught a breeze during this program and actually transformed it into an audible message, including communications from the departed. Could a tree somehow amplify discarnate energies and convey them as important messages? That possibility was illustrated by a student who heard her deceased father's voice clearly congratulating her as she meditated alone under an oak tree on the day of her graduation from college. Another student whose teenage brother had been recently killed in a traffic accident insists she heard him whisper her name as she meditated under an elm tree. The experience was for her a comforting manifestation of her brother's safe transition to the other side.

Even a small indoor tree can be an important empowerment resource. Aside from brightening almost any home or office setting, it can stimulate conversation and promote positive relationships. In group therapy, the sheer presence of a live, indoor tree can promote therapeutic interactions. In couples counseling, the presence of a tree seems to facilitate communication and reconciliation. On the recommendation of their therapist, a couple on the brink of divorce together selected an indoor tree for their home as a symbol of their relationship goals. In the words of the husband, "The tree opened a new door that brought us together and saved our marriage."

In another application of the indoor tree, a high school teacher intern introduced a tree as a still-life model for her art class. At the end of the internship, student evaluations of the intern's performance rated the tree project as among their most valuable and unforgettable learning experiences.

THE EXTENDED POWER OF TREES

Given the relevance of trees as important empowerment resources, it requires no quantum leap to conclude that certain parts when removed from the tree could retain at least some of the tree's empowerment potential. It should come then as no surprise that personal empowerment programs occasionally incorporate small fragments taken from trees as links to the parent tree. One not uncommon practice holds that even a seed or small piece of bark removed from the tree and carried in the pocket or purse as reminders of one's commitment can provide the motivation or inspiration required to achieve a designated goal. These practices, when augmented with a strong expectancy effect, have demonstrated unusual effectiveness for an array of personal goals, such as quitting smoking, losing weight, overcoming stage fright, building feelings of worth, and improving social relations. Many of my students report having successfully used this strategy to accelerate learning and improve their test performance.

Another approach called the *Center of Power* consists of arranging seeds from a plant or tree in a geometric design on the ground or other flat surface, and meditating at its center to connect oneself to sources of power both within oneself and beyond. The seeds are usually designated as representing a particular goal, typically by stroking the seeds while stating your goal as you form the geometric design, such as a circle, triangle, or star. Once the design is formed, meditating at its center while focusing on the designated goal is thought to access the resources required to achieve it. This simple approach seems to facilitate a spontaneous energy surge that powers up the imagination and expands awareness to totally new possibilities.

Although any seed or geometric arrangement can be used for the Center of Power, the seed of a persimmon tree arranged in a five-point-star design is often preferred because of its purported receptivity to higher dimensions of power. It was while meditating at the center of a persimmon seed star that a college student experienced for the first time a compassionate spirit presence who would guide her out of an entangled relationship. In her words, "I felt instant relief as if a weight had been lifted." The experience was a turning point that gave her a new sense of personal power and well-being. In another instance, a graduate student coping with grief following the sudden loss of both parents in a traffic accident experienced their comforting presence while meditating at the center of a persimmon seed star. By his account, the experience led to a deeper understanding of their deaths as a wondrous transition rather than a tragic ending.

Not unlike seed and bark, leaves are a principal component of the tree as Earth's antennae to the universe. Working in concert, they've been known at times to manifest energy by their unexplained rustling even in the absence of a breeze, a pattern illustrated by Phoenix, as earlier discussed, when he appeared to disperse healing energy to an injured dog.

Because leaves are essential to the survival of trees, their energy properties seem to be second only to those of the tree itself. The leaf of a tree is the tree's signature and its outer reach. Once you've established an interaction with the tree, you can sense its energizing qualities by simply stroking its leaf. Even when removed from the tree, the leaf's shape and patterns identify the tree from which it was taken.

As it turns out, the fragile leaf can become a highly operative manifestation of the tree, and in some instances, an important link to the power of nature. Though it may seem extreme to some, there are reports of the leaf as having worked alone as if influenced by an unseen higher force. For instance, the mother of a hospitalized child reported that a colorful leaf drifted slowly as with purpose into her car when she lowered the window upon entering the hospital's parking tower. By her account, the appearance of the leaf signaled a turning point in the child's recovery. The leaf was, in her view, "nature's testament of a healing presence."

THE CRUMPLED LEAF

The *Crumpled Leaf* is a simple step-by-step empowerment program based on the premise that a leaf, when removed from a tree, retains its energized connection to the parent tree and from there, to the universe, a concept that gains credibility through a phenomenon known as the "phantom leaf effect." That effect has been repeatedly demonstrated in our labs through electrophotographs of a leaf after a portion of it had been cut away. With the end section of a leaf missing, repeated photographs of the remaining leaf, even with a different photographic apparatus, consistently revealed images of the full leaf. That effect was also noted in the photographs of a flower petal when a portion of it had been removed, a phenomenon I call the "phantom petal effect."

The Crumpled Leaf is designed to promote an empowering interaction with the leaf and the tree from which it was taken. The interaction is then expanded to include the universe at large. The lowly leaf—if we could call it lowly—turns out to be a functional gateway to the universe. Here's the program.

Step 1. Tree Selection

Select a tree with leaves that can be easily and safely crumpled. Place your hands upon its trunk and sense its unique features, a gesture that recognizes the tree's interactive capacity. Think of the tree as an extension of your own energy system and your partner in the use of this procedure.

Step 2. Leaf Selection

Having initiated an interaction with the tree, select a leaf that commands your attention. Carefully remove it from the tree, and gently hold it between your palms with its topside up and its stem pointing toward yourself. Think of the leaf as your connection to the tree, and the tree as your connection to the universe.

Step 3. Crumpling the Leaf

Crumple the leaf into a mass as you would a sheet of paper before throwing it away. Notice the energizing effects of briefly holding the crumpled leaf in your hand.

Step 4. Interpreting Leaf Patterns

Carefully unfold the crumpled leaf so as, if possible, not to tear it. Examine the leaf, paying careful attention to its patterns and lines, to include geometric designs. Take plenty of time to allow thoughts and feelings to emerge as you examine the unfolded leaf.

Step 5. Empowerment Applications

To initiate an empowerment interaction with the leaf, place it again between your palms, and, with your eyes closed, sense its energies interacting with your own energy system.

Remind yourself that the leaf is your connection to the tree, and from there, to the universe. As your interaction with the leaf builds, note your sense of renewal and personal empowerment.

Step 6. Goal Statement (Optional)

At this point, you may wish to state a personal goal and engage the leaf as your interactive partner of power. As the leaf remains between your palms, visualize your goal and verbally affirm your commitment to achieve it. For this exercise, the sound of your own voice can become a powerful force that assures your complete success.

Step 7. Conclusion

Conclude by either returning the leaf to the Earth or placing it in a secure place for future reference. You may wish to place it between the pages of this book.

In a rather unusual application of this approach, an engineer who was conducting research on energy used the crumpled leaf in his effort to develop advanced, energy efficient alternatives. For the exercise, he selected a wind-blasted leaf from an aged oak on the laboratory grounds. Although the leaf sustained several tears when crumpled, he placed the unfolded leaf between his palms and stated his goal. At once, detailed images of a totally new technology appeared vividly in his mind. He developed the technology that became recognized as a major advancement. The framed leaf, titled "Super Tech," is prominently displayed at the research facility in honor of its important contribution to energy research.

Along a different line, awareness of a guiding presence in Step 5 of the program is not uncommon. At that step, the leaf resting between the palms seems to facilitate a merging of dimensions, at times with important healing relevance. A teacher whose teenage son had sustained a serious head injury in a motorcycle accident experienced upon placing a crumpled poplar leaf between her palms a warm pulsation. By her report, "I immediately experienced the comforting presence of a higher force." The experience signaled the beginning of her son's complete recovery.

In yet another instance of possible merging of dimensions, a pre-law student experienced while holding the crumpled leaf between her hands the gentle presence of her parents who had recently died in a small plane crash. According to the student, she actually heard her mother whisper her name. She found reassurance through this simple technique that life continues beyond death in a rich, wondrous dimension, rather than in some cold, distant place.

In the clinical setting, the Crumpled Leaf as a therapeutic approach tends to promote communication and generate a positive therapeutic interaction. When used as a projective technique in which patients interpret their own leaf patterns, the crumpled leaves can uncover subconscious elements with highly significant therapeutic implications. This approach is also useful in couples' counseling in which partners interpret each other's crumpled leaf patterns.

SUMMARY

Trees are Earth's oldest and largest living things, but they are far more than that. They are among our most valuable links to the powers of nature. Through our interactions with them, we can access new growth resources within ourselves and beyond. We have yet to discover the empowering limits of this magnificent creation.

4: the power
of the forest

It makes all the difference whether one sees darkness through the light, or brightness through the shadows.

—DAVID LINDSAY

If a lone tree can become a functional link to the hidden side of nature, imagine the possibilities of an old-growth forest. Simply viewing a magnificent forest from a distance can inspire us by its splendor and beauty. A closer interaction with the forest regardless of the season can connect us to vast new sources of power.

I discovered early in life that interacting with a primal forest could generate mature self-assurance and an attitude that's conducive to growth and progressive change. I will always remember a certain winding forest trail near my home where I often walked during childhood and well into my teens. At each side of the trail's entrance and arching over it were two large elms that formed a graceful gateway. These mystical trees seemed to whisper, "Life is beautiful," as you approached them. Just beyond the elms were several huge oaks with clusters of mottled, weather-worn leaves. Standing steadfast, they were like old, trusted friends you could always count on. Near a shallow brook crossing the trail, an exceptionally large holly tree with polished leaves and bright red berries added a festive flourish to the trail. Just ahead, several enormous sweet gum trees joined star-shaped hands over the trail to form an emerald arch that filtered the sunlight and radiated inspiration. I always lingered in the bright green glow to soak in its exhilarating energy. Adding to the appeal of the trail were the intermittent cedars that freely dispersed their refreshing fragrance. Near the end of the trail stood a group of tall pines that carpeted the trail year-round with their slender light-brown needles. Finally opening upon the airy splendor of a vast meadow beyond which lay yet another primal forest, the trail ended with bold confirmation of my lifelong philosophy that the best is yet to come.

While the nature walk in almost any setting can be empowering, hiking along a mountain wilderness trail can be especially rewarding. Breathing in the high-altitude air can be a pressure relief valve that brings the mind, body, and spirit into full attunement. A few years ago, I conducted a nature walk with a group of my psychology students in a dense, old-growth forest in middle Tennessee. It was fall and the leaves had taken on the brilliant colors of a painter's palette. The oak's bold earth hues, the maple's bright yellow tinged with light green and shades of red, and the sweet gum's rich maroon created a striking canvas of natural beauty.

With my students a considerable distance ahead, I entered an open area encircled by magnificent maple trees. The early afternoon sunlight filtering through golden leaves bathed the opening with a rich, magical glow beyond anything I'd seen before. Briefly lingering in the autumnal glow, I breathed in the fresh air and experienced an unforgettable sense of complete oneness with the universe. Like the early sphere craft experience of my childhood, it was a moment of power at its peak.

Although I would never return to that special place, I would time and again re-live the experience in vivid imagery, always with the same wonderment of that resplendent moment many years ago.

THE NATURE WALK

While structured procedures may not always match the splendor of a spontaneous moment, they can provide the essential conditions required to access new power and target it needed. The Nature Walk is a step-by-step, goal-oriented program designed to achieve that important goal. It recognizes the forest as a valued empowerment resource and gateway to self-empowerment. It facilitates a positive interaction with the forest that builds feelings of worth and self-assurance while balancing and bringing into harmony the mind, body, and spirit. It's a goal-oriented approach that focuses on designated goals and builds an unwavering determination to achieving them.

In a forest area where there are no marked trails to follow, practicing this program in the company of a partner or group can add security to the experience and minimize the possibility of losing your directions. When used with others, joining hands before and after the walk as a positive expression of purpose can provide interactive enrichment to the experience. Give yourself plenty of time for the program which is designed for use during daylight hours. With appropriate planning, this structured program as follows is effective for use in almost any secure forest setting.

Step 1. Formulate Your Goals

Prior to the walk, formulate your goals, limiting them to no more than three, and affirm your commitment to achieve them. Think of the forest as an enormous repository of energy that's receptive to your stated goals, which can range from simply experiencing the serenity and beauty of the forest to such diverse objectives as better health, self-insight, and career success.

Step 2. Select a Forest

Select a safe forest setting with a trail for the walk, preferably in the company of a partner or group that can add both protection and interactive enrichment to the walk.

Step 3. The Walk

Upon entering the forest area, pause briefly to experience its splendor by sensing its sights, sounds, and smells. Take time to calm your mind as you breathe in the fresh forest air. Sense the forest's energies merging with your own to permeate your total being. As you walk deeper into the forest, soak in its peace and tranquility. Notice the richness of the forest and let yourself experience the renewal and inspiration that typically accompany the walk. Periodically pause at highly energized points to reflect on your goals. Take time to form goal-related images and let them go forth, perhaps navigating among trees to gather the energies required for your complete success.

Step 4. Listen to the Forest

Throughout your walk, pause periodically to listen to the sounds and unspoken messages emerging from deep within the forest. Think of them as embracing your presence and a confirmation of your future success and fulfillment.

Step 5. Conclusion

Upon completing the walk, turn your hands toward the forest in recognition of its empowering relevance as you affirm in your own words your complete success in achieving your goals as specified in Step 1.

Once you've completed this program, you can reactivate its rewards at will by simply taking time to visualize the forest and reflecting on your interactions with it. Rather than fading with time, our past interactions with nature become even stronger as we reflect on them. They are sources of power that are available to us at will.

The therapeutic effects of this program can be worth hours of psychotherapy. For couples, it's an excellent way to open new communication channels and find solutions to relational problems. According to one couple, "It was a major breakthrough—we were finally able to talk, really talk." Overcoming depression, reducing stress, building self-esteem, and staying in shape are all within the scope of this program.

As a therapeutic approach, this program recognizes the forest as a natural therapist. By providing therapeutic interactions with nature in a safe forest setting, the program can be a critical source of personal growth and fulfillment. It's an action method that can be used as an important component for both individual and group therapy.

SUMMARY

Starting now, you can give new hope and meaning to your life by interacting with nature through its forests. As an interactive partner, the forest can bring you into harmony with nature and put you in touch with your higher self. Whether simply viewing a magnificent forest from a distance or engaging it close-up, the forest can enrich your life and inspire you to reach your highest goals. If a tangible forest is unavailable, you can use visualization to create a forest of your own.

When your future is uncertain or life seems meaningless, your interactions with the forest can give direction to your life and open exciting new pathways for growth and self-discovery.

5: the power
of plants

There are more things in heaven and earth,
Horatio, than are dreamt of in your philosophy.
—WILLIAM SHAKESPEARE, *HAMLET*

Can you imagine a planet without plants? A world without plants is like a sunset without color—stripped of its splendor and beauty.

Being a tree person, I'll admit I've never seen an unattractive plant or tree. They're like the human aura, that colorful energy field enveloping the physical body. I've yet to see an aura without beauty.

Flowering plants with their natural beauty and engaging aroma are an especially amazing work of nature. Even the prickly pear with its yellow blossoms and pear-shaped fruit is a magnificent creation to behold. Aside from its singular beauty and edible fruit, it speaks forcefully of independence and survival against all odds. From the climbing honeysuckle to the unassuming bitter weed, the foliage, flowers, and smell of plants are splendid testaments to nature's power and beauty.

Increasingly, plants across cultures have taken on important spiritual significance as reflected by the meditation or faith garden. Given the beauty, energy, and serenity of plants, imagine the good things than can happen when plants and people come together in a tranquil garden. What better place for a world peace conference than a peaceful garden setting!

As a psychologist, I discovered early in my practice the therapeutic value of plants. In both indoor and outdoor settings, plants can enrich the therapeutic process, whether for individuals, couples, or groups. Plants by their sheer presence can lift the spirit and literally disperse healthful energy. In the therapeutic setting, they are like co-therapists that specialize in restoration and fulfillment.

The outdoor garden setting is especially effective for such quality-of-life goals as quitting smoking, managing weight, staying fit, or remaining young. For quitting smoking, simply taking a few moments to breathe fresh outside air deeply into the lungs can help extinguish the need to inhale smoke. Following that with slow, rhythmic breathing of fresh air accompanied by positive affirmations of yourself as a non-smoker can break the smoking habit once and for all. Periodically reminding oneself that breathing in fresh air is far more healthful and satisfying than inhaling smoke can add to the pleasure of being a nonsmoker.

For losing weight, the sights, sounds, and smells of the outdoor setting when accompanied by imagery of yourself weighing the exact amount of your stated goal can empower you not only to lose weight, but to keep it off. You can strengthen your resolve as needed by simply walking among plants and observing their beauty while reaffirming your success in achieving your goal.

In the educational setting, plants can open totally new pathways for growth and self-discovery. Learning specialists know that the nature of the environment can profoundly influence the rate of learning while promoting retention of the material learned. For my students, I've found that outdoor class sessions, even if only sporadic, tend to stimulate interest and participation, regardless of the subject matter. Beyond that, the outdoor instructional setting can dramatically facilitate the positive transfer of learning, in that what is learned in the outdoor setting is much more readily applied to other life situations.

As in academia, the outdoor setting has special implications for the health professions. Many enlightened physicians and psychologists alike now recognize the importance of the health-related resources found in nature, including the indoor and outdoor meditation garden. Doctor/patient interactions do not take place in a vacuum—they are strongly influenced by the setting in which they occur. Taking time to wheel patients outside the hospital room and interact with them at eye level in a garden setting can dramatically increase the patient's feelings of worth while improving the effectiveness of treatment. For the terminally ill, it can enrich the quality of life in its ending stages. Hopefully, physicians of the future will increasingly utilize nature's healing resources, including the meditation garden, not only for patients and their families, but for themselves as well.

THE PLANT INTERACTION PROGRAM

One of the simplest, yet most powerful plant-related approaches, is the *Plant Interaction Program*. This program embraces the familiar concept that big things can have small beginnings. Through this step-by-step program a lone plant can become a gateway to complete success. By focusing your attention on a plant, you can access the resources required to achieve your highest goals.

The effectiveness of this program seems to lie primarily in its capacity to generate a highly motivated state with strong expectations of success. Developed in the college setting for instructional enrichment, the program seems to actually shape the mind for success. It is applicable to a wide range of personal goals, from the simplest to the most complex, but for only one goal at a time. It can be practiced in almost any setting where a plant is available for viewing. Here's the program.

Step 1. Goal Statement

Formulate a specific personal goal and affirm your intent to achieve it in clear, positive terms. For instance, the affirmation, *I will succeed,* is far more powerful than the affirmation, *I will not fail.*

Step 2. Observation

Select a plant that seems relevant to your stated goal and center your attention on it. Note the plant's distinguishing characteristics, such as texture, size, and color. Remind yourself that plants, life, and people, are unique, with no two being exactly alike.

Step 3. Plant Visualization

Close your eyes and visualize the plant in as much detail as possible. As you build a mental image of the plant with its unique features, sense your connection to it as a magnificent creation.

Step 4. Goal Visualization

Shift your attention from the plant to your goal. Again, state your goal and visualize yourself having achieved it. If, for instance, your goal is career-related, picture yourself in a career situation that's consistent with your stated goal. Think of your visualized goal as a future reality poised for fulfillment.

Step 5. Plant-goal Connection

Return your focus to the plant and think of it as nature's symbol of your success in achieving your goal. Let the reality of the tangible plant represent the reality of your future success. Take plenty of time to form a firm *plant-goal connection*.

Step 6. Concluding Affirmation

Conclude with the simple affirmation, "Success is my destiny." You can use this affirmation as a cue at any time to reactivate in an instant the full effects of this program.

For multiple goals, repeat the program for each goal. This program is especially effective when practiced in the early morning hours. It's a good way to start your day!

PLANTS AND THE AFTERLIFE

Let the skeptics say what they will—there exists an abundance of evidence suggesting the relevance of plants to the afterlife. Reports concerning plants, especially flowers, as messengers that confirmed life beyond death are common. What could more appropriately signal afterlife survival than the beauty and fragrance of flowers?

The flower as an afterlife messenger was dramatically illustrated by a college student who awakened in the night to see a glowing image of her recently deceased grandmother standing at the doorway to her dormitory room. Clutching a bright red rose, her grandmother, who was an avid gardener, reached forward and said with a smile, "This special rose is for you." With that, she faded into the night, leaving behind the light fragrance of roses. While the experience alone was profound, it took on added meaning a few days later when the student received a bright red rose from her grandmother's sister, also an avid gardener, with the same message: "This special rose is for you." For the student, the two events brought joyous confirmation of her grandmother's continued life and love beyond death.

Yet another instance of flowers as possible confirmations of afterlife survival is the recurrent fragrance of lilacs often noted in the president's mansion at Athens State University. Over many years, residents along with guests reported having experienced the delicate fragrance of lilacs throughout the antebellum mansion, even in the depth of winter.

Like many so-called paranormal phenomenon, there are no easy explanations for this unusual phenomenon. Although the building's historical records are fragmented, early reports of a lilac-related event at the mansion offer at least one possibility. As the story goes, a young woman named Laura Belle died in one of the mansion's upstairs bedrooms following a long, painful illness in the mid-1800s. In the final stages of her illness, an arrangement of lilacs from the mansion's garden was placed at her bedside. The beauty of the plant and its pleasing fragrance took her attention away from her illness and helped ease the pain. Each day until her death, a fresh arrangement of lilacs was brought to her room. According to the story, Laura Belle was buried clutching a bouquet of lilacs. Following her death, the aroma of lilacs occasionally wafted throughout the house, a phenomenon that, as noted, continues till this day.

Could the fragrance of lilacs and the illness associated with it over 150 years ago have been so intense that it virtually imprinted or stamped itself into the building's brick and mortar? On the other hand, do spontaneous, recurrent fissures at times occur between dimensions or planes to manifest highly specific remnants or residual effects related to a particular time, setting, or event? Or could the phenomenon be best explained as simply a manifestation of the young woman's presence in spirit form, a statement of her survival in afterlife? As I've often said, discarnate manifestations seem to meet two basic human needs—our need to interact with the departed and their need to interact with us. We could add to these yet another that's possibly the most plausible of all: Our need to experience the mysterious.

An even more widely known instance of flowers as possible manifestations of life beyond death is the recurring fragrance of roses at another historic campus site, Mc-Candless Auditorium. According to legend, it was there that Abigail Lylia Burns, a rising Philadelphia actress, performed selections from Verdi's opera *La Traviata* in the early 1900s. Following a brilliant performance, she was presented an arrangement of red roses to unbounded applause, whereupon she promised to return. Unfortunately, that night, en route by horse-drawn carriage to her next engagement, she was mortally wounded when her carriage overturned during a severe thunderstorm. As the legend goes, Abigail, still clutching the red roses, was heard to say upon being drawn from the wreckage, "I've a promise to keep. I must return."

Abigail may have kept that promise. Soon after her death, the recurrent fragrance of roses accompanied by occasional sightings of the actress was noted in the auditorium where she performed, a phenomenon observed till this day, particularly on November 12, the apparent date of her death.

Adding credence to the Abigail legend are the many collectively perceived manifestations related to the legend. A few years ago in a highly publicized presentation of *La Traviata* in the historic auditorium in honor of Abigail, members of the opera theater along with the audience experienced throughout the program the unmistakable fragrance of roses, though roses were not present in the auditorium during the performance.

In yet another instance of flowers as possible messengers from the other side, an engineer and former student of mine who was familiar with the Abigail legend may have himself used the fragrance of flowers to signal his safe transition to the other side following his sudden death in an industrial accident. On each anniversary of his six-year marriage, his gift to his wife had been a corsage of gardenias, the flower she carried at their wedding. On their seventh anniversary, approximately three months following his death, his wife, along with friends who visited her that day, noticed the distinct fragrance of gardenias throughout the house, yet gardenias were nowhere present. In her words, "On what could have been a very sad day, the fragrance of gardenias was like a bright ray of light from beyond."

At the end of the day, the underlying message of discarnate phenomena seems to be the joyous continuation of life after death. We could add to that another common message of equal importance—the endless survival of love, the most powerful force in the universe.

THE GARDEN MEDITATION PROGRAM

The meditation garden, especially when plants are arranged concentrically, can generate an energy force in which the finely tuned frequencies of plants are amplified throughout the garden, especially at its center. Although simply viewing the garden from its outside can be energizing, engaging the garden's full energies usually requires a closer interaction.

The *Garden Meditation Program* is a guide specifically designed to promote that process.

The six-step program that follows can be used in almost any garden setting. While plants that appeal to you personally are especially recommended, they can consist of almost any variety, including both flowering and non-flowering. The guide can be used alone or in small groups. Although it requires no statement of goals, the program does include goal-related options.

Step 1. The Setting

Select a quiet, safe garden setting, preferably with a central meditation area.

Step 2. The Scan

Upon approaching the garden, visually scan it, noting specifically the plants that seem to stand out from the others. Note the sounds and smells as you view the garden.

Step 3. Garden Imagery

From either within the garden or at its perimeter, close your eyes and generate a detailed mental image of the garden. Take plenty of time to form the image, a process that connects you mentally to the garden as a gateway to higher sources of power and enlightenment.

Step 4. Garden Interaction

Turn your palms outward toward the garden in acknowledgement of the garden as your link to higher sources of energy and power. Notice the relaxation and serenity that accompany this step.

Step 5. Goal Statement (Optional)

At this optional step, you can state your personal goals and focus on the garden as a gateway for achieving them. Visualize your goals enveloped in bright energy. If your goal, for instance, is career success, visualize the words CAREER SUCCESS in bold block letters, surrounded by bright energy. You can then supplement that image with bright imagery of yourself in the career situation of your choice.

Step 6. Conclusion

Conclude the meditation experience by bringing your palms together as a symbol of inner balance and attunement. At this stage, you can literally disperse positive energy on a global scale by turning your palms outward and slowly moving your hands from side to side as you visualize the globe enveloped in bright light.

This is a highly flexible program with wide-ranging applications. As noted in Step 5, you can focus on achieving your personal goals, to include health and fitness. Since the meditation garden is a healthful place, it should come as no surprise that health and fitness-related needs are particularly receptive to this guide. For that application, visualize your body fully enveloped in the glow of health. At this point, you can focus on particular organs and their functions. Take plenty of time for the infusion process to reach its peak.

Chronic pain patients are almost always receptive to the garden meditation using this program. They usually experience a marked reduction in pain along with a more positive, hopeful mental state that's conducive to wellness. Along a different line, anxious and depressed persons using the program typically experience, by their own reports, a marked increase in self-esteem and a more optimistic outlook on life.

In addition to its other health- and fitness-related applications, the garden meditation program is among the most highly preferred approaches for rejuvenation. The program seems to literally jump-start the rejuvenation process, particularly when practiced either in the early morning hours or at dusk. For rejuvenation purposes, the program seems to work best when attention is focused on the solar plexus as the body's center of energy. From there, the energy is dispersed mentally to saturate the full body. For this application, think of rejuvenating energy as emerald green, the color also associated with health and fitness. For rejuvenation and other health-related purposes, frequent practice of the program is recommended.

Over the years, I've used the Garden Meditation Program as a learning exercise for students as well as a therapy component in my clinical practice. Outside my office is a garden called the *energy garden*, with an extensive range of plants, both floral and non-floral, along with a variety of rock formations and a sandstone path leading to the garden's center where benches are situated around a fountain. Lingering at the garden's center while breathing in its fresh air and listening to the sounds of the fountain can lift the spirit and infuse the body with powerful energy.

I found early on that interacting with the energy garden tends to generate a positive state of mind that becomes a healing balm. Couples who share the garden typically become more highly motivated to resolve their differences and find solutions to problems in their relationship. In family therapy, even brief interactions with the energy garden tend to open totally new communication channels. Simply lingering in the garden can be therapeutic. The garden experience becomes more than a complement to therapy—it becomes a master therapist in and of itself.

Children are almost always receptive to the energy garden experience. For many of them, the garden becomes a special place to meet animal friends, including chipmunks that hurry along the stone path and dart among bordering plants, along with birds that groom at the garden's central fountain and nest among its shrubs. Of very special interest to children are a pair of doves that annually nest in the garden and share together the feeding and caring of their young. Time and again, I've seen children so inspired by the energy garden that they emerge from it with a renewed sense of self-assurance and security.

AGRITHERAPY

The combined activity of working with soil and nurturing plants can be so therapeutic that I've given it a name: *agritherapy*. Hands-on agritherapy is applicable for almost any therapeutic goal. I've prescribed it for conditions ranging from depression to anger management. A single agritherapy session, not unlike the nature walk and garden meditation, can be worth hours of psychotherapy—it's a gift of nature that's free to everyone. It can release stress, build self-esteem, and bring you into harmony with nature. It tends to dissolve growth blockages and build feelings of adequacy and security. It can resolve relational conflicts and bring couples closer together. As one couple put it, "Our garden and marriage grew together."

It's important to note that agritherapy is equally applicable to the community vegetable garden. As a community project, the vegetable garden can have special significance—it can bring people together in a positive interaction with nature and with each other.

Constructing the Meditation Garden

Should you decide to construct your own meditation garden, an arrangement of plants in concentric circles with a central area for meditating and interacting with the garden is among the most effective designs. A variety of plants, including both annual and perennial, can add to the garden's appeal while promoting a wider range of interactions. Based on traditions, which may vary considerably from region to region, here are some examples of widely used plants and their interactive properties or symbolic significance.

Day Lily—health and fitness.
Iris—spiritual renewal and abundance.
Rose—optimism and magnanimity.
Ivy—stability and determination.
Small bordering plants—balance and protection.

Fern—comfort and well-being.
Cactus—independence and survival.
Petunia—courage and resilience.
Zinnia—practicality and efficiency.
Gardenia—stamina and rejuvenation.
Lilac—friendship and perseverance.
Impatiens—potency and productivity.
Violet—trust and hopefulness.

Because of the uniqueness of your personal preferences in plants, your interaction with a particular plant could differ considerably from that of others. A simple free-association test is sometimes useful in determining the empowering relevance of various plants as they relate to you personally. When using this approach, begin by calling a particular plant by its name, preferably while touching the plant or in its presence, and then addressing it open-endedly as follows: "You are important because…" Finish the sentence with whatever comes to mind. As earlier noted, a variety of plants increase the meditation garden's empowerment potential.

Not unlike other plants, herbal plants when arranged concentrically can generate a powerful energy force at the garden's center where their diverse energies merge to generate a synergistic effect. By meditating at that central area, you can interact with the cumulative energies of various herbal plants to empower your total energy system. The procedure can attune your energy system and infuse it with the abundant energy properties of the garden's herbal plants. The energizing effects of herbal plants seem to be greatest in the early morning hours.

Summary

Clearly, plants are so essential to our existence that it's impossible to imagine life on earth without them. By their existence alone, plants add beauty to the Earth and meaning to our existence. They are among the most abundant manifestations of the power of nature. By applying the strategies presented in this chapter, you can tap into that power to enrich the quality of your life. By interacting with plants, you can focus on specific goals and access the resources required to achieve them. Even the most fragile plant can become a profound link to nature's amazing power.

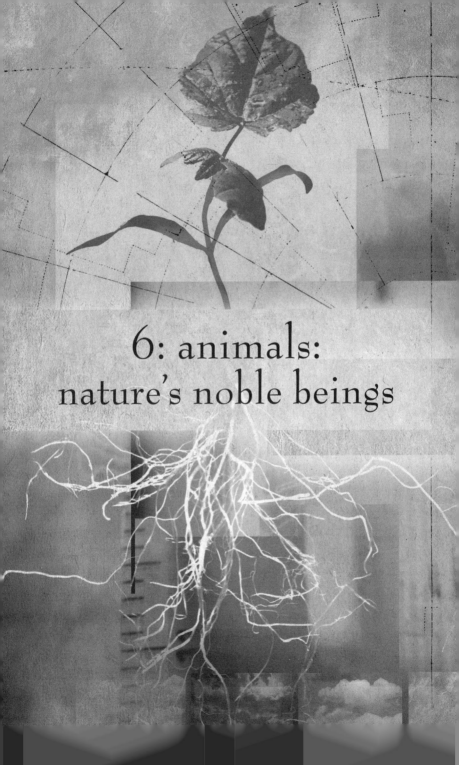

6: animals:
nature's noble beings

With all beings and all things we shall be relatives...
—ANCIENT LAW OF NATURE

As with plants, I can't imagine a world without animals—nor can I imagine life on the other side without them. It's an honor to share the planet with animals; and it will be an honor to share the afterlife with them. From a flock of geese in scripted flight to a raccoon as undisciplined as a Martian dust devil, animal beings exemplify the collective life force that energizes and sustains all living things, along with the universe at large. Together they can connect us to the essence of our being as evolving souls.

As a child, I learned at a very early age to respect all animals as conscious beings of dignity and worth. I often watched my father compassionately caring for sick or injured farm animals, always talking to them as if they understood his every word. My mother shared my father's deep respect for animals, including the abandoned and wayfaring ones that showed up at her door. She compassionately cared for them, often giving them names that fitted their appearance or personality. It was as though they bonded with her, as did she with them, on sight.

I'll admit I may have carried my parent's regard for animals to a whole new level by including even insects, not as lowly entities but as creatures worthy of respect. Growing up on a farm, I regularly visited the livestock watering troughs to free struggling insects trapped in the water. I remember once rescuing a helpless moth, its wings spread wide to stay afloat. I slipped my hand under it and carefully lifted it from the water. As it lingered near death in my palm, I felt so connected to the fragile creature that I thought, "I wouldn't want to live in a world without moths." Then, when the moth finally revived and took flight, I experienced the titanic thrill of having single-handedly saved a creature of great beauty at the edge of death. I felt as though I had made the world—at least *my* world—a better place by saving a moth.

Even insects that sting, including bees and wasps, were not excluded from my rescue efforts. They rested in my open hand, often in an enfeebled fetus-like position, until they could fly; yet never once did they sting. After recovering, they seemed to linger in my hand a little longer than other insects, a gesture I took as an expression of their gratitude.

Though I'd never heard of the transmigration of souls, it occurred to me as a child that I could have lived a past life as an animal being. Or if not a full lifetime, perhaps temporarily embodied in animal form as a transient walk-in.

Possibly in my past-life evolvement, I needed to know what it was like to be a wayfaring animal—whether furred, feathered, or bare skinned, it really didn't matter. Perhaps I could learn something by being a contemplative lizard embracing the earth and observing other life forms from below, or possibly a resilient fox embodying both brawn and brain.

It also occurred to me that my past-life existence as an animal being could have contributed to my present-life appreciation of them as beings worthy of protection and respect. It could have also influenced my choice not to kill animals for either food or clothing. Although it may seem extreme to some of my readers, I'm steadfast in my belief that subjecting animals to inhumane treatment—whether in factory-farming, the experimental laboratory, or any other setting—not only violates the rights of animals, it degrades the human spirit. I'm further convinced that disregard for the well-being of animals brings us out of harmony with nature, and on a much wider scale, impedes global progress. I remain convinced that one of the best measures of how far we've advanced as a culture rests largely in the nature of our treatment of animals.

My early interest in animals and the lessons I learned from them also included bird watching and listening to their calls. I often observed them skillfully building their nests and raising their young. I learned early in life to value diversity by observing the different lifestyles of birds—the dignity of the dove, independence of the crow, assertiveness of the blue jay, congeniality of the mocking bird, and reticence of the brown thrush, to mention but a few. I was intrigued by their beauty and wide-ranging calls that seemed to match their distinctive lifestyles.

Little did I know as a child that I would one day incorporate bird watching into my teaching and clinical practice of psychology. Bird watching requires no special training, and it's available to everyone. Through bird watching, you can get close to nature and experience the unqualified joy of viewing beings of great beauty while learning from them in their natural habitat. Simply observing and listening to birds can attune you within and bring you into instant harmony with nature. Beyond that, bird watching can add depth and meaning to your life by connecting you to that spiritual part within.

At times of personal loss, birds can function as benevolent messengers that comfort and inspire, a characteristic of these gentle beings I've personally experienced. For me, the loss was the sudden death by accident of a close family member, and the messenger was an unusual blackbird. Soon after tragedy struck, I was driving at sunrise on a bridge spanning a wide river near my home when a row of blackbirds, all perfectly aligned on the bridge's side rail, commanded my attention. As I approached the motionless birds bathed in sunlight, one near the middle of the group caught my eye—it was exactly like the others except it was *white*. At once, the white bird took flight, leaving the others behind. As I watched the bird gracefully soar, I experienced a gentle lifting of my grief and a comforting reminder that death, rather than an unfortunate end, is a wondrous new beginning—a bright gateway to another dimension of endless growth and fulfillment.

For one of my former students who is now a clinical psychologist, nature's gentle messenger was a colorful butterfly. Soon after the unexpected death of her father, she was resting at the campus pool when a swallowtail butterfly lit upon her hand. With the butterfly lingering lightly—its wings in slow, rhythmic motion—she was reminded of her seafaring father and his great love for nature. Among her fondest childhood memories were times spent with her father viewing the seascape at sunset with multicolored clouds stretching across the sky. He believed in the endlessness of life and the oneness of all creation. Her one regret was not being with him at the time of his sudden passing. When the butterfly finally took easy flight, she felt, in her words, "an almost imperceptible tug as though a gossamer thread had broken." Simultaneously, she sensed the loving presence of her father and a complete release of all grief. It was an unforgettable moment of power at its peak.

For a professor colleague stricken with grief over the death of his young son following a long illness, nature's unlikely messengers were fireflies at dusk. While watching the fireflies from the back deck of his home as night fell, he was reminded of another night on the same deck when his son brought for his inspection a jar of several fireflies he had just caught. Before releasing them, his son insisted, "It's time to let them go. Fireflies need to be free." Together, they watched as, one by one, the fireflies, no longer trapped in the jar, escaped their confinement and took easy flight to join other fireflies lighting up the night. Now alone on the deck as night deepened, he felt the gentle presence of his son, no longer trapped by pain and illness but free to fly and light up the night sky. He knew it was time to let the grief go.

Summary

Earth's magnificent creatures, both large and small, are living manifestations of the unseen side of nature. As beings of dignity and worth, they exemplify the dynamic life force that energizes our existence and sustains all things, both seen and unseen. They enrich our lives with new insight and offer comfort in times of adversity and personal loss.

Unfortunately, a species, when challenged by the environment, is not always able to come up with a solution. It's then left to us to take action. In protecting the environment and caring for threatened or endangered species, we discover the rich rewards of nurturing life and making the world a better and far more beautiful place for present and future generations.

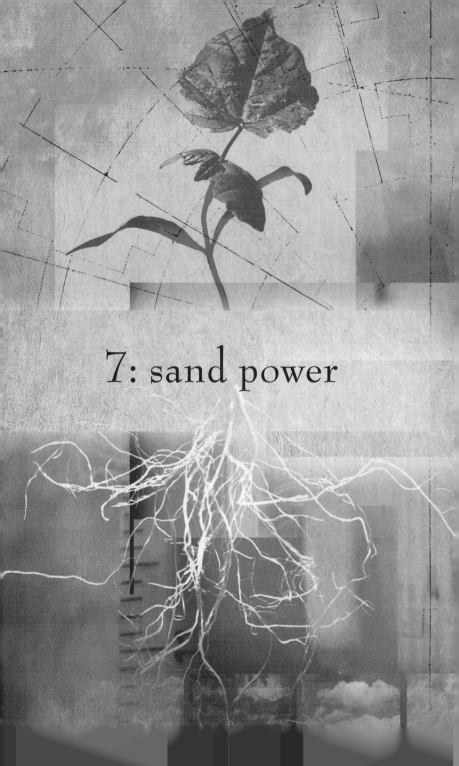

7: sand power

We have seen the highest circle of spiraling powers.
We have named this circle God.
We might have given it any other name we wished:
Abyss, Mystery, Absolute Darkness, Absolute Light,
Matter, Spirit, Ultimate Hope, Ultimate Despair, Silence.
—NIKOS KAZANTZAKIS

From the sandbox to the sandbar, sand is among Earth's most abundant resources. Aside from its abundance, sand is so essential to the planet that if it were somehow removed, the earth's beaches and deserts alike would disappear. Without their sand components, even great castles and cathedrals would crumble and fall. It should come then as no great surprise that sand-related empowerment strategies are among the most effective known.

Almost everyone can recall early childhood experiences related to sand. My very first memory is that of playing in sand in the dappled shade of a great oak tree. Sand-related activities tend to foster healthful mental growth and change—not only during childhood, but throughout life. A walk along a sandy beach, for instance, can generate at any age a state of oneness with nature and balance within. Add to that the glittering beauty of the seascape and the empowering possibilities of sand become even greater.

THE FLOWING SAND PROGRAM

My early childhood experiences with sand, including simply holding sand in my hands and allowing it to flow through my fingers, would became years later the seminal inspiration for the *Flowing Sand Program*. The program recognizes the self-empowering possibilities of simply allowing sand to flow gently through your fingers. That simple experience tends to spontaneously clear the mind, reduce stress, banish insecurity, and create a more positive outlook on life. It tends to attune the mind, body, and spirit in an instant while generating strong feelings of being in charge of your life and destiny.

The Flowing Sand Program is designed to maximize the effectiveness of that experience which can reach far back into childhood. Based on the concept that *complexity seeks simplicity*, the step-by-step program holds that complex mental functions tend to be receptive to the simple sensations generated by sand flowing slowly through the fingers. The program is structured so as to put you in charge. By merely holding sand in your cupped hand and deliberately regulating its flow through your fingers, you can experience the intrinsic rewards of the procedure while building the self-confidence and determination required to achieve a wide range of personal goals.

The simple program can be implemented in almost any setting where dry sand is available. I often use it with a sample of sand from the Great Pyramid of Giza, a gift from a former student. Here's the four-step program adapted for use indoors with a small tray of dry sand.

Step 1. Goal Statement

Formulate a specific goal and identify, if possible, a reasonable timeline for achieving it. For instance, if your goal is to complete a certain project, describe the project and target a completion date. If your goal is career success, specify your criteria for success.

Step 2. Sand Interaction

Take a handful of sand from the tray, and while holding it in your cupped hand over the tray, restate your goal. Let the sand then begin to flow slowly through your fingers into the tray. Note the sense of security and balance generated by the flowing sand. Affirm that the flowing sand represents your progress toward achieving your stated goal as relevant images of success form in your mind.

Step 3. Hand Press

Once the sand has returned to the tray, place your hand upon the sand and press firmly, a gesture that signifies your strong resolve to succeed. With your hand pressing upon the sand, sense your interaction with the sand as you affirm in your own words your unwavering determination to achieve your stated goal.

Step 4. Handclasp of Power

Conclude the exercise by simply bringing your hands together in a firm handclasp as you affirm: *I am now fully empowered to achieve this goal.* You can use this simple cue called Handclasp of Power at will to activate in an instant the full effects of the program.

The Flowing Sand Program can be used for almost any personal empowerment goal. It's especially effective for breaking unwanted habits, extinguishing phobias, mastering complex mental and physical skills, ensuring academic and career success, and managing stress. For breaking unwanted habits, think of the sand in your hands as the habit itself, and the sand flowing through your fingers as the release of that habit. Think of the hand press gesture as your power over the habit. For quitting smoking using this program, the instant "cold turkey method" is recommended over the tapering down approach. Use the Handclasp of Power as a post-program cue as needed to ensure your complete success.

For extinguishing a phobia, think of the handful of sand as the fear, and your regulation of the sand as it flows through your fingers as your progress in releasing it. Think of the hand press (Step 3) as confirmation of your liberation from fear. Use the handclasp as needed to assume instant command over any threatening situation.

For acquiring a complex skill, such as mastering a new language or technical skill, think of the sand in your hands as that skill and the sand flowing through your fingers as your continuous progress in achieving it. Let your hands pressing upon the sand represent your firm resolve to master that skill. As with other applications, you can use the Handclasp of Power as needed.

The Flowing Sand Program is particularly useful in academic and career settings. When practiced prior to a test or important conference, it can increase mental efficiency, reduce negative stress, and generate self-assurance. A pre-med student who had assisted in our development of the program decided to use it in her effort to gain admission to medical school. Her approach was two-fold: Immediately prior to the required admissions testing, she used the program to boost her mental functions, and throughout the long test session, she used the handclasp cue as needed. She attributes her high score and subsequent acceptance to medical school, in large part, to the Flowing Sand Program.

Another student used the program prior to an important job interview to reduce stress and increase her self-confidence. During the interview itself, she used the inconspicuous handclasp cue to, in her words, "put me at ease and keep me focused." The simple cue, by her admission, "worked"—it gave her the winning edge required for selection to the position.

In the career setting, the Flowing Sand Program with its post-procedure cue can help you stay energized and connected to today's career lifestyles. It can generate zest for your work and a positive attitude for career growth and productive change.

As earlier noted, you can use the flowing sand exercise independently of structured procedures and fixed goals. It's especially effective as a spontaneous relaxation and stress management strategy. Simply regulating the flow of sand through your fingers demonstrates your ability to control external events. It's a reminder that you can deliberately intervene in real-life situations to influence outcomes. The result is a stronger sense of internal control over your life and the events that influence it.

From another perspective, letting go of the sand in your hand can be seen as a metaphor for eliminating whatever is holding you back in your life. Allowing the sand to flow freely through your fingers can dissolve blockages and releases stress, frustration, insecurity, pressure, hostility and other disempowering forces that could interrupt your life and thwart your growth. When you're stressed out with the volume turned up, this simple exercise not only provides release, it generates security and mature self-assurance that can enrich the quality of your life.

Interestingly, any program that reduces stress tends to spontaneously spawn important insight, to include that of subconscious origin. In one of my recent seminars titled *Self-empowerment Through Nature*, a space research engineer practicing the Flowing Sand Program experienced a fleeting image of an advanced self-correcting design that would require no backup system in case of equipment failure. The simple technique of allowing sand to flow through her fingers, in her view, spontaneously activated the subconscious faculties required to generate awareness of the advanced design and convey it to consciousness in visual form. We could conclude that even our most complex mental faculties seek simplicity.

SAND READING

Sand reading is an approach that uses the handprint, palm side down, on the surface of moist sand as a focal point and potential source of important new information. Sand reading recognizes our hands as our body's antennae with diverse interactive functions. The handprint is seen as a visible representation of those functions. Given the concepts of handwriting analysis, fingerprinting, and palm reading, it seems only plausible that a handprint could likewise hold important relevance as an information source.

The only material required for sand reading is a tray of sand large enough to accommodate the full hand, including the fingers when in a spread position. The sand is usually moistened slightly so as to retain an accurate handprint. To make the handprint, simply place either hand, palm-side down, on the smooth surface of the sand and press gently into it.

Sand reading can be administered to oneself or to another person. When administered to others, the instructions can vary, but usually consist of the following: "Simply place your hand, palm-side down, on the sand and make a handprint in the sand." For repeated handprints, the surface of the sand is smoothed after each trial using the straight edge of a card.

Controlled observations have repeatedly authenticated sand reading as a potential source of information not readily available through other methods. Here are a few examples.

- Analysis of the handprints of college students revealed fingers in a typically closed position immediately before a course examination; whereas immediately after the examination, the fingers tended to be spread apart. These results suggested the usefulness of sand reading in detecting stress associated with situational factors.

- Among inmates in a prison setting, greater depth of the handprint was typically noted for violent offenders compared to non-violent offenders.

- Regarding gender differences, males tended to press their hand at greater depth in the sand than females; however unemployed males tended to make handprints of less depth when compared with employed males. Employment status among females did not appear to influence the depth of their handprints.

- Comparisons of the handprints of plumbers versus dentists tended to differentiate those vocational groups, with dentists showing greater variation in their handprint orientations. Compared to dentists, plumbers in our study showed greater depth in their handprints and more space between the fingers.

- In the psychiatric setting, the handprints of patients were often slanted and oriented to the left of the tray. Depressed as well as anxious patients used very light

pressure to produce very shallow handprints with little or no space between the fingers.

Although these findings are considered tentative, they do
suggest that sand reading, given additional research, could
become an effective way to assess a variety of personal characteristics. As we'll see, however, personal assessment is only
one of the many possible applications of sand reading.

CLINICAL SAND READING

In the therapeutic setting, sand reading using a small tray
of sand has shown interesting clinical applications. *Clinical
Sand Reading*, as it's called, can be used to establish a positive relationship while yielding important information of
therapeutic relevance. This approach seems to be especially
effective when used with adolescents and young adults,
particularly as a projective technique in which subjects view
their own handprint and describe what they see in it. For
that application, the person's description and interpreta-
tion of the handprint are discussed in a non-judgmental,
supportive manner that focuses on personal perceptions
and feelings. Using this approach, the subject often projects
onto the sand important personal characteristics of psychological relevance. Here are a few examples of the therapeutic possibilities of clinical sand reading.

- A high school sophomore who projected her feelings of
  inferiority and social rejection onto her handprint began working on ways to build her feelings of adequacy
  and self-worth. During counseling, she was introduced

to the Flowing Sand Program and began using it to effectively release stress and increase self-confidence.

- A college student with an obsessive need for perfection experienced difficulty producing a handprint that met his approval. After several attempts, he pushed the tray aside in exasperation. The experience motivated him to explore his exaggerated need for perfection and eventually resolve the conflicts related to it.

- A couple undergoing counseling used sand reading in their efforts to reconcile their differences and strengthen their relationship. The strategy, which included interpreting each other's handprints, led to better communication and a deeper understanding of their relationship.

CREATIVE SAND READING

Sand reading can provide a useful focal point for generating new ideas and insight of important personal relevance, both for the present and future. For that application known simply as *Creative Sand Reading*, you can use your own handprint or that of another person. Here are the suggested steps for that application.

Step 1. Obtaining the Handprint

Obtain a handprint using standard sand reading procedures in which a handprint of either hand, palm-side down, is formed in sand.

Step 2. Viewing the Handprint

View the handprint, whether that of yourself or another person, paying particular attention to specific details, such as orientation of the hand, depth of handprint, and position of fingers. Remind yourself that the energies required to form the handprint remain in the sand to sustain it.

Step 3. Expanding Awareness

Place your hand slightly above the handprint and clear your mind of all active thought. Note the impressions and mental images that spontaneously unfold. It's at this point that profound new insight will often emerge, to include impressions of present and future relevance.

Step 4. Conclusion

Conclude the exercise by turning the palms of your hands upward to balance and attune your energy system, a gesture you can also use as a post-procedure cue as needed.

A student using creative sand reading experienced in Step 3 what seemed to be the past-life source of his combined fears of heights, darkness, and enclosed places. With his hand resting over the handprint, images of himself falling while mountain climbing and becoming hopelessly trapped in a dark, deep crevice vividly unfolded like a movie in his mind. As the images slowly faded, he sensed also the fading of all fear. For him, a flash of past-life awareness was all it took to unleash the insight required to extinguish a trilogy of phobias that had plagued him since childhood. A simple handprint provided the essential link that liberated him from fear—yet another reflection of the two-fold concept: *Complexity seeks simplicity and enlightenment is power.*

As noted in Step 4, you can, at will, turn your palms upward as a post-procedure cue to balance and attune your energy system in an instant. It's often during this gesture that additional insight of highly practical relevance will emerge. As an example, it was during this gesture that a psychology doctoral student experienced detailed concepts that inspired his dissertation research on the physiology of cognition. In another instance, a political candidate experienced word for word a campaign slogan that, in her opinion, gave her the winning edge in her bid for office.

In the group setting where pairs of subjects work together, creative sand reading can be used as a strategy to promote more positive, productive social interactions. Sharing impressions related to handprints can stimulate discussion and open the interactive channels required for such activities as brainstorming, planning, creative thinking, and problem solving. The program is especially recommended for newly formed groups once they are appropriately oriented.

AUTOMATIC SAND WRITING

A variation of creative sand reading is *automatic sand writing*. Similar to standard automatic writing, automatic sand writing spontaneously provides new information using the fingertip and sand rather than pen and paper as writing materials. This approach is based on the premise that information previously unavailable to conscious awareness can emerge effortlessly and automatically through sand writing. The source of the information, according to this approach, can be from either within oneself or beyond.

For automatic sand writing, you can use either open-ended or directed sand writing. For the open-ended approach, simply rest your index finger lightly on the smooth surface of sand and allow it to write automatically in the sand. Initially, the writing may appear as unintelligible scribble, but soon meaningful information will almost always emerge.

For directed sand writing, the finger, again resting lightly on the sand, writes in response to specific questions to provide "yes" or "no" answers as well as other written messages. In a somewhat dramatic example of this directed sand writing, a graduate student attempted using this method to identify the name of the person she would eventually meet and marry. In answer to her question, "What's the name of my future husband?" her finger wrote in the sand the name *Alan*. There was, however, a minor error in the message. The person she would later meet and marry was named *Allan*. Another college student, a sophomore majoring in pre-law, used the procedure to accurately identify the law school she would later attend.

Like most other empowerment approaches related to nature, automatic sand writing is highly flexible. The sand used can be any surface of sand, and another writing tool can be substituted for the finger. A college student enrolled in a creative writing course used automatic sand writing with a sharpened twig as a quill and the beach as a scroll to compose an assigned short story in the moist sand. Upon completing the story, which included both open-ended and directed writing, he hastily copied it from the sand just before an ocean wave erased it. He submitted the story to his professor who gave it an excellent rating with the one-word notation, "Brilliant!" I read the story and agreed with the professor. The story was promptly published in the school's journal, but without mention of its origin as a product of automatic sand writing.

Aside from written compositions, automatic sand writing can produce highly creative designs, a function illustrated by a celebrated artist who frequently uses it to generate new ideas for his works. As he put it, "What better way to produce a work of art than to use a creative strategy to give birth to it?"

Together, a creative composition and an artistic design produced in sand offer further proof: Complexity seeks simplicity.

Summary

The power of sand is authenticated—it's a concept whose time has come. Simply allowing sand to flow gently through your fingers can engender feelings of serenity and balance. Placing your hand upon the sand, even in a laboratory tray, can connect you to new sources of insight and knowledge. Simply viewing a handprint in sand as a point of focus can generate awareness of significant present and future relevance. Writing with your finger as a pen and sand as a scroll can automatically activate the mind's creative powers and generate important new products of subconscious origin.

As it turns out, one of nature's most abundant resources is also one of its most powerful.

8: the power of water and rocks

To trace the history of a river or a raindrop…
is to trace the history of the soul,
the history of the mind descending and arising in the body.
In both, we constantly seek and stumble on divinity…

—GRETEL EHRLICH

Without water, Earth would be a barren, hostile place. Water is so fundamental to our existence that early on it was interwoven into our identity as a nation situated in beauty from sea to shining sea. Further reflecting the early cultural relevance of water is the important historic role of the Nile in ancient Egypt and the development of water-powered technology by the early Romans. Putting out to sea or crossing a river has long been used metaphorically in poetry and song to signify death as a spiritual voyage to a distant shore.

The sights and sounds of water—a rushing mountain stream, a crashing waterfall, an intoxicating moonlit cove, a fresh snowfall, a vast ocean, a glacier that scrapes the sky—

can be peak experiences that connect us to ultimate reality and the divine nature of our being. From walking in the rain to navigating rapids, interactions with water can infuse the mind, body, and spirit with abundant new energy and power.

The sea is among the many sights and sounds of nature that can become a wondrous source of inspiration and power, particularly when we encounter mortality at a deeply personal level. For a college student struggling with grief following the sudden death of her fiancé, a spectacular seascape became the turning point in her recovery. As she walked at sunset along the beach as she had often done with her fiancé, the Earth and sky took on a rich golden radiance as the sun sank beyond the sea. Caught by the stunning beauty of the scene, she sensed the unmistakable presence of her fiancé and a gentle lifting of her grief. In her words, "It was as though we were together again, walking hand-in-hand at sunset along the beach." For her, the splendor of the sea at sunset signaled with certainty the continuity of life and love beyond death in a dimension of indescribable beauty.

For a young executive charged with a serious crime he did not commit, it was a freshly fallen snow in the moonlight that brought resolution and relief. In his despair, he had considered suicide as a last resort. Stepping outdoors onto the blanket of snow, he was struck by the sharp contrast between the hopelessness that gnawed within and the sparkling splendor of the scene that stretched before him. At that moment, he sensed a comforting "spiritual embrace," as he called it, along with the gentle lifting of his despair. He knew without a shred of doubt that the accusations against him would be resolved—and they were. Within days, the guilty party came forth and admitted to having committed the crime.

As a young boy, I discovered that even a farm pond could become an enormous source of power. There was something almost magical about the crystal clear pond situated just beyond the tree called Phoenix. It was fed by the everlasting spring called Rock Fountain as previously mentioned. Even though I had an early fear of water, I often visited Crystal Pond to dangle my feet into it from a weathered pier. It was finally through a vividly detailed dream that I discovered what appeared to be the source of my fear—a past life in which I drowned in the Mediterranean at an early age. Awakened in the night by the impact of that insight, I was certain that my fear of water had vanished. I could hardly wait to visit Crystal Pond. A few days later, with my two brothers looking on in disbelief, I dived right in for the first time, totally free of fear.

It was around then that I developed an interest in rock collecting. I would soon discover that by merely tossing a rock into the pond with clear purpose, I could accomplish almost any goal. Rocks were plentiful in the area where I grew up, so I quickly accumulated a large collection, some with highly unusual characteristics. I once found a golf-ball-size rock with very distinct facial features, including eyes, nose, and mouth. The mysterious "face rock," as I called it, inspired my search for other specimens with unique features.

Soon afterward, I found a crest-shaped rock that I carried for years in my pocket as a good-luck piece. When Midnight, my beloved cat of many years, died, I unearthed a star-shaped rock while digging his grave in the burial plot we had set aside for companion animals that had crossed over. My father mounted the grayish star against black in a shadowbox frame with the title: *Midnight Star.* The framed star hangs today in my office, not only in memory of Midnight, but also as a reminder of my father's great love for animals. He firmly believed in the afterlife of animals, and as mentioned earlier, he always treated them as beings of great dignity and worth.

Although I had long collected rocks, I first became aware of their empowering relevance at age twelve, when my best friend was killed in a traffic accident. It was after school on a late Friday afternoon when tragedy struck. On the school bus, we had made plans for the upcoming weekend, which included riding horseback and swimming in Crystal Pond. He had just exited the bus at his home when an oncoming car struck him as he crossed the road. He died instantly.

In the days that followed, my grief over the death of my best friend at that young age only increased. Finally, I decided to do something in his memory. I went to my collection of rocks and selected one we had found together. It was an unusual rock, possibly a fossil, in the shape of a wheel with a hub and definitive spokes. I had heard my grandmother speak of the "wheel of life," and the brownish yellow rock reminded me that my friend's life was on going. I decided to toss the rock into Crystal Pond. Fed by the everlasting spring, the pond, like the wheel, seemed to be a logical representation of the endlessness of life.

On an early overcast Saturday morning, I went alone to Crystal Pond with the small rock in hand. When I tossed it into the glassy smooth water, I felt an instant and complete release of grief. But more importantly, I experienced a calm awareness of my friend's presence. I knew at once that he was safe on the other side. I also knew for the first time that the other side, rather than some strange, distant realm to be feared, is a peaceful place as close as the air we breathe. I actually felt that I could reach out and touch it. I experienced first hand the full wonder of a dimension from which we all came and to which we would all return. A special stone tossed into a crystal clear pond was all it took to change grief into peaceful acceptance. Beyond that, a stone cast into water brought forth at that early age a deeper understanding of the interrelatedness of dimensions and the endlessness of life. Though I would continue to miss my friend, I at last shared with him the joy of his life on the other side.

After that profound experience, I continued adding rocks to my collection, including numerous unusual pebbles I collected from a nearby stream. Though worn smooth by water, each pebble was unique in size, shape, and color. Once upon tossing a bluish pebble into the water, I realized that each pebble is also unique in the ripples it forms as it enters the water and the path it takes as it sinks to the bottom. It occurred to me that by simply tossing a pebble—any pebble—into water, I could create a unique energy event, the like of which had never occurred before nor would ever occur again.

The Pebble and Pond Program

My early experience with pebbles and water was to become years later the seminal inspiration for a step-by-step program called *Pebble and Pond Program.* The program is based on the premise that a simple natural phenomenon can possess significant empowerment potential. The program's only required resources are a common pebble and a pond or any other body of water. For multiple goals, the full program with a different pebble is recommended for each goal. Here are the essential steps.

Step 1. Goal Statement

Specify your goal, stating it in positive terms. Think of your goal as a future reality in the process of fulfillment.

Step 2. Pebble Selection

Select a pebble to represent your stated goal. As the pebble rests in your hand, note its unique features such as weight, shape, texture, and color. Remind yourself that the pebble you hold in your hand is unlike any other pebble.

Step 3. Pebble Interaction

Stroke the pebble gently and sense your interaction with it. As you continue to hold the pebble, affirm: *This pebble represents my goal of* (state goal)*; and this pond represents my determination to achieve it.*

Step 4. Pebble Toss

Toss the pebble into the water and notice the ripples it creates. Think of the ripples as your ability to overcome any obstacle or opposition to your goal strivings. Think of the pebble's descent as your deepening resolve to achieve your goal. Think of the pebble's final resting place as your destiny for complete success.

Step 5. Concluding Affirmation

Conclude the program with the assertion: *I now have all the resources and determination required to achieve my goal of* (specify goal). *I will succeed. Nothing can stop me now.*

The Pebble and Pond can be used for almost any self-development goal, including breaking unwanted habits, resolving conflict, solving personal problems, enriching social relationships, and building feelings of security and self-worth, to list but a few. For these applications, think of the pebble as representing your goal with the pond representing the mental resources required to achieve it. Let the pebble entering the water represent the activation of the required resources, both conscious and subconscious. Think of the pebble at rest in the pond as representing the continued activation of those resources, including the deepest powers of your subconscious. You can present relevant affirmation throughout and after the procedure to reinforce its effects. Examples are: "I am destined for success. Once I decide to do something, nothing can stop me. I now have all the resources I need to succeed."

As with almost all personal empowerment programs, the relevant use of mental imagery can dramatically increase the effectiveness of the Pebble and Pond Program. For example, if your goal is to lose weight, picturing yourself standing before a full-length mirror weighing the preferred amount not only motivates, it activates the inner resources required to achieve that goal. Similarly, if your goal is to quit smoking, picturing yourself being offered a cigarette and simply saying, "No, I'm a nonsmoker," can build your resolve and ensure your complete success.

The Pebble and Pond Program is a highly flexible approach that can be easily revised to meet your personal preferences and the demands of wide-ranging situations. A former student, for instance, used an adaptation of the program to gain admission to law school. He selected a pebble from the law school's campus to represent his application, and a campus fountain to represent the law school. Standing at the fountain's edge, he affirmed, "Just as this fountain is receptive to this pebble, this law school is receptive to my application." He then tossed the pebble into the fountain, whereupon he affirmed, "I will be admitted to this law school." A few days later, the law school notified him that he had been unconditionally accepted for admission.

The Pebble and Pond Program can be readily adapted for use by groups. In team sports, for instance, a revised procedure called the *Pebble and Pail Exercise* has been effectively used to energize players and building team spirit, usually just moments before an athletic event. After appropriate orientation, each player tosses a pebble into a pail of water typically located in the locker room. For this application, the pebble represents determination, the water represents potential, and tossing the pebble into the water represents team accomplishment. The expectancy effect generated by this exercise can be a decisive factor in almost any competitive sports situation.

The fact that athletes usually find the exercise amusing seems only to add to its empowering effects.

Another adaptation of the Pebble and Pail Program met unprecedented success when used by a church group to launch an ambitious building program. After a silver tray of pebbles and a punchbowl-like vessel of water had been placed side-by-side at the church's altar and blessed by the rector, the members one-by-one pledged their commitment to the building effort by selecting a *Pebble of Commitment* from the tray and dropping it into the vessel of water called the *Vessel of Faith*. The vessel of faith with its pebbles of commitment is prominently displayed in the church's magnificent new sanctuary as a testament to commitment and faith.

THE WELL OF PROMISE

In the rural southern community where I grew up, there's an old but still-popular ritual called the *Well of Promise*. According to the ritual, you can get a fleeting reflection of the person you will eventually meet and marry by looking into an old water well, preferably a hand-dug well. By then tossing a small pebble into the well to seal the future relationship, you can ensure a successful marriage. No one seems to take the ritual too seriously, yet there are many reports of both men and women who claim to have first glimpsed their lifelong mate by looking into an old well.

The ritual, it seems, is not limited to the rural south. One of my former students, now a college professor, reports that the practice has a long history and remains popular in her hometown in the Northeast. By her account, almost no one believes in the ritual, but it's hard to find in her small hometown anyone who hasn't practiced it. She admitted that she as a teenager once looked into an old well to see reflected in the water an image remarkably similar to the person she would later meet and marry. But by her admission, she did not toss a pebble into the well to seal the relationship, and the marriage did not last.

The Bottomless Pool Ritual

It's a fact—marriages, like other relationships, do not always last. While the divorce rate has declined in recent years, the numbers tell us that still over a third of new marriages end in divorce. An ended marriage, however, does not necessarily indicate a failed marriage. Some relationships simply run their course, and some actually improve after a disengagement or divorce. Bringing the relationship to a satisfactory close can be the best solution for a relationship that is no longer viable. But even when ending the relationship is the preferred option of both partners, residual effects can persist. Resolving past conflicts and letting go of any negative baggage associated with an ended relationship can be a difficult needle to thread.

Deep in a popular southern forest reserve known as Bankhead Forest, there's a so-called bottomless pool that has been for many years the site of an interesting ritual claiming to promote successful disengagement or closure when a relationship or marriage ends. The *Bottomless Pool Ritual*, as it's called, consists of casting your wedding band or other important article associated with a relationship into the pool and then washing your hands in the pool's water. Casting the object into the water symbolically disengages the relationship and dissolves any connection to it, whereas the washing of hands in the pool represents a release or cleansing of all residual effects of the past relationship. After tossing his wedding band into the water, a graduate student who was enrolled in my class went so far as to dive into the pool to become completely free of a relationship he described as "hopeless." He said it worked!

A few years ago, a young attorney whose marriage had ended in divorce decided to visit the bottomless pool and perform the ritual, but with some unexpected consequences. As he approached the pool, he saw at its edge an exquisitely beautiful woman who was there also to throw her wedding band into the water. By his report, they connected instantly and together cast their rings into the water. He recalls, "I found the love of my life at a bottomless pool."

Because the pool is so deep and usually considered a somewhat hallowed place, there are no reports of efforts to salvage any of the articles cast into it.

THE DISENGAGEMENT TOSS RITUAL

The *Disengagement Toss Ritual*, not unlike the Bottomless Pool Ritual, is designed to facilitate disengagement in a nonviable relationship and promote resolution of its residual effects. The step-by-step ritual is based on the premise that tangible items can embody psychic energy or substance with long-term interactive properties. It would follow that a wedding band signifying marriage can assume psychological meaning commensurate to the past history and present state of the relationship. As an interactive symbol of the relationship, the ring can continue to embody the memories and emotions associated with the relationship long after it ends. The Disengagement Toss Ritual is designed to extinguish any disempowering interaction with the ring. Furthermore, through disposing of the ring rather than passing it on to another person, you can theoretically prevent any transfer of its negative properties. Here's the ritual.

Step 1. Setting
With the ring in hand, find a body of water of considerable depth, such as a river or lake.

Step 2. The Toss
Immediately before tossing the ring into the water, affirm: "With the tossing of this ring, I do hereby disengage the relationship it represents and any baggage it may carry." With an upward fling, toss the ring into the water.

Step 3. The Release
Close your eyes and note your sense of freedom from the past relationship and complete release of all baggage related to it.

Step 4. Conclusion & Post-procedure Cue
Conclude the procedure with the bold affirmation: "I am now fully empowered." You can use this affirmation at any time as a post-procedure cue to reactivate the empowering effects of the full procedure.

As with the Bottomless Pool Ritual, any piece of jewelry or other small article associated with the ended relationship can be used for this procedure when a wedding ring is not available.

THE STREAM OF POWER

You may have never thought of a mountain stream as a personal empowerment resource. I am, however, including it here because of its unusual effectiveness when used to energize the mind, body, and spirit, and bring them into a state of balance. The *Stream of Power* uses meditation with imagery of a mountain stream to generate a positive, optimistic state of mind that increases feelings of adequacy, security, and self-worth. While the presence of a stream is not required, the background sound of water in motion can enhance the effectiveness of this four-step meditation program.

Step 1. Preliminaries

As you listen to (or imagine) the relaxing sounds of water in motion, settle back and take in a few deep breaths, exhaling slowly. With your eyes closed, give yourself permission to become increasingly relaxed and free of tension by mentally scanning your body from your forehead downward.

Step 2. Visualization

Clear your mind and visualize a mountain stream tumbling over rocks and pressing ever forward. Think of the stream as representing the life-force energy flowing throughout your total being. Let the innermost part of your being become illuminated with bright energy as all barriers to your growth slowly dissolve away. Let this process continue until it seems to have run its course.

Step 3. Goal Power

With your mind, body, and spirit in a state of harmony and balance, turn your attention to your personal goals—both immediate and long-range. Use visualization to give mental substance to your goals and affirm your power to achieve them. Think of the stream as your inner stream of power, capable of overcoming all obstacles.

Step 4. Conclusion

At this concluding step, again visualize a mountain stream as in Step 2, or you can use the following meditation guide, which is suitable for recording.

I AM THE STREAM

I am the stream of progress. Emerging from deep caverns, I am flowing forward into the light of new knowledge, ever expanding my range of awareness and understanding.

I am the stream of enlightenment. Settling into placid pools of serenity, languishing to reflect in the shade, I gather my resources before once again pressing forward to explore, search, and discover my innermost being, overcoming all obstacles to my progress and growth.

I am the stream of success. Steadily flowing among towering trees of aspiration and winding among boulders of inner strength, I am revitalized and attuned to the positive energies of the universe. My destiny is success and greatness.

I am the stream of peace. Gently flowing into the sunlit valley of peace, I am calm, confident, and secure as I advance steadily to join the illimitable sea of universal oneness.

I am the Stream as a meditation guide can be used independently of the full program to facilitate visualization and create a success orientation that's relevant to any goal. Even against great odds, the expectation of success can be a formidable force that generates the persistence and commitment required for complete success.

Water Gazing

Water Gazing is a program developed in our labs to stimulate a variety of complex mental functions and promote their further development. A major benefit of Water Gazing is the "spherical glow effect" and the resulting state of inner balance and renewal.

Water Gazing uses a spherical, clear glass container filled with water as a convenient point of focus to clear the mind and generate a relaxed, receptive state that's conducive to higher mental functions. The bowl of water is usually positioned on a table to facilitate a comfortable eye-level gaze. Here's the procedure.

Step 1. Preparation
With a clear, spherical bowl of water situated on a table to facilitate easy gazing, close your eyes and take in a few deep

breaths, exhaling slowly. Develop a slow, rhythmic breathing pattern and let yourself become increasingly relaxed, beginning at your forehead and spreading slowly downward throughout your total body.

Step 2. Clearing

Open your eyes and center your attention on the bowl of water. While focusing on the bowl, slowly expand your peripheral vision to its limits by viewing as much of your surroundings as possible, to each side of the bowl, above it, and below it. As you hold that expanded view, let your eyes shift slightly out of focus, and you will notice a white glow called the spherical glow effect, first around the bowl and then throughout the room. Notice the relaxation and serenity that accompany this phenomenon.

Step 3. Focusing

Return your focus to the bowl of water and resume gazing. Sense the activation of your higher mental faculties as images, impressions, and insights unfold. Take plenty of time for this state of expanded awareness to run its course.

Step 4. Conclusion

Close your eyes and sense the balance and renewal that always follow focusing. Affirm in your own words your ability to use the insight and knowledge gained through this experience to achieve your highest goals and enrich the quality of your life.

Water Gazing, while originally developed for use individually, can be easily adapted for use by groups once they have been appropriately oriented. In the group setting it can generate positive interactions and facilitate such activities as brainstorming, problem solving, and creative thinking. For these applications, the bowl is usually situated at the center of a group seated in a circular arrangement. Gazing occurs in brief segments, with impressions and ideas shared after each segment.

Summary

The sights and sounds of water, from a raindrop to a singing waterfall, can connect us to the innermost part of our being and the life force that energizes our existence. As we've seen, simply tossing a pebble with purpose into a pool of water can unblock barriers that thwart our growth and inspire us to achieve our highest goals. Rituals related to water can facilitate recovery and resolution when relationships fail or become nonviable.

At a deeply personal level, many of my fondest memories are centered on water. Tossing a special pebble into a farm pond in memory of a friend, meditating to the sounds of water springing forth from Rock Fountain, and diving into a pool to celebrate my liberation from a childhood fear of water remain till this day firmly etched in my mind as manifestations of the magnificent power of water.

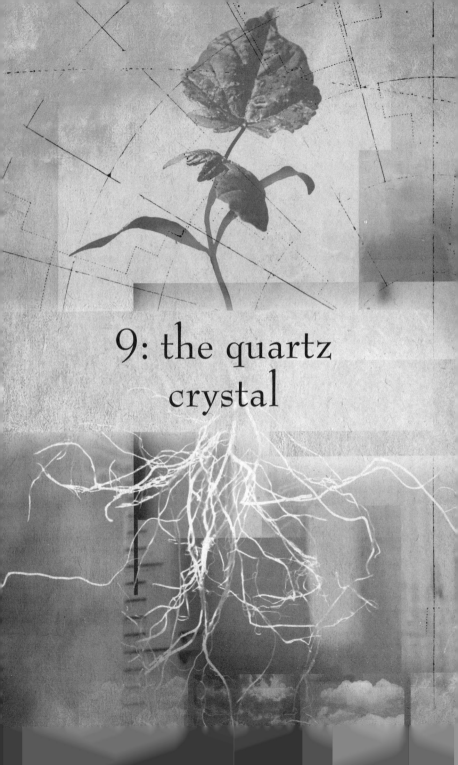

9: the quartz crystal

It is the greatest joy ... to have explored the explorable and
then calmly revere the inexplorable.
—Johann Wolfgang von Goethe

It's estimated that on average we develop only about a tenth of our mental potential, and while not everyone would agree, that's probably an overestimate. In undeveloped form, our potential is like a butterfly trapped in a jar. With its wings folded and actions constricted, the butterfly offers only a limited glimpse of its exquisite grace and beauty. But once liberated from entrapment, it spreads its wings and ascends in wondrous splendor.

Freeing the trapped butterfly of possibilities by developing our mental powers to their fullest is one of life's greatest challenges. Fortunately, we are surrounded by nature's resources that, by design and function, are constantly poised to facilitate that process. Among them is the quartz crystal.

The quartz crystal is widely recognized as a natural resource of both beauty and power. Consisting of a silicon dioxide in colorless or slightly tinged hexagonal form, it can be worn as an ornament, carried in the pocket or purse, or displayed in crystalline masses as a decorative object. Aside from these, it is often valued for its capacity to generate, store, and send energy along with its high receptivity to programming, an interactive procedure we'll later discuss.

While the origin of quartz crystal is unclear, one theory holds that Atlantis, upon its demise, seeded the earth with the crystal as a benevolent contribution to the betterment of the world. Another view posits that the quartz crystal was introduced to planet Earth by advanced extraterrestrials who understood its potential to promote the evolution of the globe and the betterment of humankind.

Whatever its origin, the quartz crystal has increasingly gained acceptance as a crystallized embodiment of energy with near-unlimited applications. When appropriately programmed, it has reportedly been known to sharpen the intellect, unleash creativity, promote wellness, facilitate rejuvenation, improve social relationships, promote career success, break unwanted habits, extinguish phobias, protect from danger, improve memory, and even access higher dimensions of knowledge and power. Aside from these, the quartz crystal can be more generally programmed for such applications as meeting the unanticipated demands of any situation or simply enriching the quality of one's life.

Although there's an expanding body of research suggesting the empowerment possibilities of interacting with the quartz crystal, first hand experience remains the most convincing evidence. I was personally introduced to the quartz crystal at an early age by my grandmother, a gracious and talented woman whose amazing feats included driving—or perhaps better put, piloting—a horse-drawn carriage through thin air over a flooded stream and breaking up threatening clouds by wielding an ax overhead and vigorously thrusting it at an angle into the ground, along with many other amazing skills as discussed in my book, *Beyond Reincarnation* (2006). I can't be sure of what role the quartz crystal played in these remarkable accomplishments, but I do know she called it her "empowerment companion." I never saw her without the crystal she wore as a necklace pendant. When my younger brother fell on a broken bottle and cut a deep gash on his lower arm, my grandmother rushed to his side. Compassionately bending over him, she quickly stroked the crystal pendant with both hands and then placed one hand against his chest and the other at his back. Almost instantly, the bleeding stopped. Next, she placed one hand under his arm to support it and the other over the open wound but without touching it. She then began what we would today call an aura or energy massage. After a few circular movements of her hand over the wound, again without touching it, she removed her hand, leaving only a thin line where the deep gash had been.

Afterward when I asked how she had stopped the bleeding and closed the wound so quickly, she would only repeat what I'd heard her say often before, "Some things we learn in this life; some things we learn after this life; and some things we learn before this life. It doesn't matter when we learn them, it's how we use them that counts."

Like her many amazing feats, the origin of the clear, double-terminated quartz crystal my grandmother wore would remain a mystery—she would only say that it came to her long ago as one of several in a collection. I would later see the collection on an overnight visit to my grandparents, who lived only a few miles from my home. It was in the depth of winter as we gathered after dinner around a roaring fireplace in the parlor. With the leaping shadows from the crackling logs dancing across the floor, the conversation turned to the recent illness of Tess, the horse that always drew my grandmother's carriage. My grandfather, a veterinarian, had been treating Tess with conventional methods, but with little success. That's when my grandmother stepped in. To accelerate Tess' recovery, she situated a quartz crystal under the horse's feeding box, a logical place, it seemed, since the horse's illness involved digestion symptoms. The crystal, however, was more than just another crystal. My grandmother had selected it from her collection and specially "inscribed" it, a procedure similar to what we would today call "programming." She had first cleared the crystal and then mentally inscribed it as a healing agent specifically for Tess. Tess' recovery was rapid and complete.

As the evening wore on, my grandmother opened a large, hidden compartment in the parlor's old cylinder desk to reveal a magnificent collection of quartz crystals of various sizes, displayed on black velvet. I immediately felt connected to them all.

That night ,with the house quiet, I looked out the window of my upstairs bedroom to notice it had begun to snow. Falling slowly in the still night air, the snowflakes, larger than any I'd seen before, reminded me of quartz crystals against black velvet. I imagined that perhaps one day I would find a quartz crystal to add to my growing collection of rocks.

THE RAINBOW CRYSTAL

A few weeks later, I again visited my grandparents as I often did on weekends. It was like *déjà vu*. Gathering as before around the parlor's roaring fireplace after dinner, I knew that I would once again view the crystals. As I looked on, my grandmother opened the desk's secret compartment with its assortment of crystals and said, "One of these crystals belongs to you." She then invited me to pass my hand over the assortment and select a crystal of my own. I chose a special crystal I had noticed upon first viewing the collection. Small enough to be carried in my pocket, the otherwise colorless crystal had an unusual inclusion in the form of a pyramid with rainbow coloration.

Until this day, the rainbow crystal, as I call it, remains in my keeping, a treasured reminder of that night long ago. Over the years, I've worked with it—and it with me—not as merely an object, but a valued empowerment resource. In some instances, the crystal proved to be a generous partner when programmed for specific goals; at other times it seemed to have worked alone—totally independent of programming.

THE STAR CRYSTAL

Nothing occurs by happenstance. A second crystal, as if by destiny, entered my life when at seventeen I enrolled in the University of Alabama as a freshman. On the day before registration, I anxiously arrived for the first time on campus by bus around midnight. Immediately upon stepping from the bus on the dimly lit University Avenue, I saw a bright object on the ground directly in front of Denny Chimes, a historic campus landmark. It was a colorless quartz crystal with a highly unusual inclusion in the form of a luminous star. Instantly upon picking it up, I knew with certainty that I was at the right place at the right time! Endowed with two crystals—the rainbow crystal from childhood and now this one from out of nowhere—I felt at once doubly empowered with each crystal working in harmony with the other.

The "star crystal," as I called it, was to become a valued companion and instrument of power throughout my college years. Because I'd discovered it on campus, I thought of it as my academic companion. I programmed it time and again for goals involving a variety of research and academic efforts. It was in fact, in my pocket when I appeared before an exigent doctoral committee for the final defense of my doctoral dissertation. While always receptive to programming, the crystal seemed to have a perpetual program of its own—it always went beyond its programmed limits to bring enrichment like a ray of sunlight into my life, regardless of the situation.

Finally, at commencement with the star crystal in my pocket, I knew that its mission in my life was accomplished.

That night, I returned to Denny Chimes where the special crystal had first entered my life. While sitting on the steps of that tall landmark with a full moon rising above the trees and the crystal in hand, I recalled that night a few years before when, upon stepping from a bus, the crystal shining in the moonlight had caught my eye, as if to welcome my arrival. I remembered having picked it up to experience an incredible connection to it that would continue throughout my college years. I reflected on how the star crystal had enriched my life as a student from the start. I recalled how I had interacted with it to accelerate my mastery of a second language, one of the requirements for my doctoral degree. It was there to inspire my research efforts, which ranged from studies of problem solving in preschool children to the rejuvenation and longevity secrets of centenarians. Though I still can't explain it, the crystal had been in my pocket when a neatly folded one-hundred-dollar bill mysteriously appeared in the same pocket just when needed to meet an emergency. It had been in my pocket, along with the rainbow crystal, when I barely avoided a head-on collision with a car that crossed over into my lane on the busy University Avenue.

As these and other images flooded my mind, I knew in an instant what I had to do. It was by then around midnight, the same hour the star crystal had entered my life. I stroked it one last time and with deeply mixed feelings, placed it on the ground where I'd found it. I walked away but couldn't resist looking back to see it shining in the moonlight more brilliantly than I'd ever seen it before.

Before leaving campus early the next morning, I revisited Denny Chimes, but almost as expected, the crystal was nowhere to be found. Could it have already embarked on another mission, perhaps to inspire yet another anxious entering freshman? Given its incredible powers, I thought, "Why Not?" I never saw the crystal again.

CRYSTAL PROGRAMMING

Although the quartz crystal can be spontaneously empowering, especially when it enters your life unexpectedly as was the case with the star crystal, its functions can be deliberately designated and focused on specific goals by formally programming it. Through appropriate crystal programming, you can establish a personal interaction with the crystal that effectively activates and targets its powers. As noted earlier, you can program the crystal for highly specific objectives or for more general purposes such as promoting the quality of your life or meeting the demands of unexpected life situations.

A major step in crystal procedure involves clearing the crystal of any previous programming, a strategy that formats the crystal for new programs. I prefer the term "clearing" rather than "cleansing," as is often used, because clearing does not imply negative properties. To assume that the crystal has negative or impure properties can complicate clearing. I have yet to find a crystal with negative or impure characteristics. A natural resource of incredible beauty, the crystal is a positive instrument. As such, it is receptive only to positive programming. Any effort to program the crystal for negative purposes will have a boomerang effect—it will return with disempowering forcefulness.

The following step-by-step guide for crystal programming is designed to initiate a positive, goal-oriented interaction with the crystal.

Step 1. Goal Statement

Formulate your goals, limiting them to no more than three to promote easy focusing. Think of your goals, not simply as possibilities, but rather as future realities awaiting fulfillment.

Step 2. Selecting a Crystal

In selecting a quartz crystal from an assortment, pass your hand slowly over the crystals without touching them. You may sense your own energies interacting with those of the crystals. It's important to select a crystal that appeals to you personally. Not infrequently, it will be the crystal that commanded your attention upon first viewing the assortment. Although quartz crystals vary in color, size, and clarity, the nature of your interaction with the crystal is far more important than the crystal's physical features.

Step 3. Clearing and Formatting the Crystal

Before specifically programming the crystal with your personal goals, it's essential not only to clear the crystal of any past programs, but also to format it for new programming. To both clear and format the crystal, simply hold it briefly under warm (not hot) running water while stroking it gently, and then place it on a towel of natural fiber, such as cotton, to air dry. Another effective clearing and formatting strategy requires stroking the crystal briefly as it soaks in rainwater and then allowing it to air dry, again on a towel of natural fiber.

Step 4. Programming the Crystal

To program the cleared, formatted crystal, hold it in your hand and while stroking it gently, engage it in your own words as a receptive instrument of nature. With your eyes closed and the crystal resting in your hand, state your goals, again limiting them to no more than three and using visualization whenever possible. Sense the receptivity of the crystal as your own energies merge with those of the crystal to become a powerful force in your hand. Save the program by simply saying, "Please stay."

Step 5. Conclusion

To conclude programming, again stroke the crystal in recognition of its receptivity to your stated goals.

When programming a crystal, I routinely include in the procedure a provision that the crystal's functions are not limited to those I've specified, a technique that implies trust in the programmed crystal, along with recognition of its extensive range of powers. Unanticipated situations, including those for which we may be unprepared, do arise. It's reassuring to know that a programmed crystal is at hand to empower and protect us as needed. For whatever the nature of the programming, the crystal is typically more effective when kept close by, possibly in your pocket or purse or worn as an ornament, and placed on a bedside table during sleep.

I've personally used the programmed crystal, at times in conjunction with other procedures, for a wide range of objectives, including establishing the Parapsychology Research Foundation, securing research contracts, and funding scholarship programs.

Strange as it may seem, the crystal once programmed has been known to disappear as if on a mission of its own, only to return when the mission is complete. A few years ago, I programmed a crystal to assist in an effort to secure a U.S. Army contract to study the human energy system at Athens State University. The specially programmed crystal, with its single terminated end and pyramid inclusion, was then placed upright on a shelf in the university's experimental lab where the study would be conducted. Mysteriously, within a few days the crystal disappeared. When the contract was finally awarded, the crystal inexplicably returned to its reserved space in our lab where it remained for the duration of the landmark investigation. The technical report for that study is now on display in the library archives at Athens State University. The crystal with a new program is presently at work promoting the Parapsychology Research Foundation's endowment and development programs.

Along a different but equally important line, there are reports of a quartz crystal being successfully programmed to guide the return of lost animals, an application that illustrates the remarkable diversity of this amazing instrument. In a recent instance, a group of my students, upon completing a wilderness hike, programmed together a crystal to guide the safe return of a student's dog that had become lost on the hike. On the second day, the dog showed up at the student's home, a distance of around twenty miles from the forest site.

Further illustrating the crystal's diversity is its apparent receptivity to business and career-related goals. The founder of a highly successful technology firm, for instance, displays on a credenza in his office a large mass of amethyst crystals that he associates with his company's rapid growth. He had carefully programmed the collective mass when the business was first formed to promote its growth and long-term success. In another instance, a highly successful attorney regularly carries on her person a specially programmed crystal that, in her opinion, empowers her to more effectively represent her clients. She attributes her outstanding success as a defense attorney, at least in part, to the specially programmed crystal. While the programmed crystal is typically kept close at hand, it can be buried at the base of a selected tree to amplify its programmed energies and disperse them more widely or else target them on specified goals. That strategy works best when combined with the Tree Power procedure as previously discussed. The resultant synergistic effect of the combined procedures can be a powerful force that ensures success, even for extremely difficult goals. In my private practice, I've used this approach as an effective auxiliary with the active participation of my clients for treatment of various conditions, including depression, chronic pain, and anxiety disorders.

Over the years, many of my students have buried programmed crystals at the base of Hercules, that magnificent tree on the campus of Athens State University, as earlier discussed. For such goals as improving their academic performance, gaining admission to graduate school, and finding employment, I know of no instance of failure when the Tree Power procedure was supplemented with an appropriately programmed crystal buried at the tree's base. I've concluded that when the crystal and tree work together, nothing is beyond their combined powers. That may seem extremely optimistic, but I've found that optimism complements the programmed crystal and actually increases its effectiveness.

Another option for increasing the crystal's effectiveness consists of tossing the programmed crystal into a stream or pool of water. Water, like the tree, seems to amplify and disperse the crystal's programmed energies. This option is especially recommended for goals related to personal relationships. An appropriately programmed crystal within the context of water seems to help bring a relationship into a healthier, more fluid state. When the programmed crystal and water work together, arrested or dormant relationships tend to take on new life in which relational conflicts are resolved and differences are reconciled. The results are enrichment and new growth in the relationship.

When a programmed crystal is to be buried or tossed into water to amplify its powers, I recommend programming a second crystal that is kept on one's person or in close proximity.

OTHER STONES

Our focus in this chapter has been on the quartz crystal because of its uniqueness and pronounced receptivity to programming. Our discussion would, however, be incomplete without a consideration of other stones and their applications. Although they are usually considered to be nonresponsive or resistant to programming, certain gemstones are believed to possess certain empowering attributes.

The empowering attributes assigned to gems, however, can vary widely among authorities and traditions. As a result, the best guide to the usefulness of a particular gem as an empowerment resource seems to rest in the nature of your interactions with that gem. As you work with gems, note your interactions with them and select gems that seem to work with you.

The following examples of gems and their applications are presented here as suggested possibilities only.

Mined Emerald. This gem is often valued for its age-defying properties. Simply wearing the gem as a ring or pendant while occasionally stroking it is thought to activate its rejuvenating capacity.

Amethyst. This gem is often associated with both mental and physical health. Wearing the amethyst is thought to generate a positive mind/body interaction that releases stress and promotes a serene state of mind. Simply holding this gem between the hands is thought to promote balance and attunement of mind, body, and spirit.

Topaz. The topaz is frequently associated with fortifying the immune system. Establishing a partnership with this gem by wearing it and occasionally stroking it is thought to activate its healthful attributes.

Sapphire. Love and affection are often associated with this gem. Simply holding the sapphire in your hand and allowing it to interact with your own energy system is thought to promote a positive emotional state.

Diamond. The diamond, the hardest substance in nature, seems to be associated with few if any empowering qualities. To the contrary, wearing the diamond is often associated with a depletion of energy and chronic fatigue. Diamond earrings in particular are often thought to slow mental functions and accelerate physical fatigue. While the diamond rejects programming, it unfortunately seems to be receptive to negative baggage, particularly that associated with failed relationships.

Among other popular stones are the tiger-eye, a yellowish to grayish brown stone that's often associated with mental efficiency and agility; the moonstone, a translucent feldspar of opaline luster often associated with magic and mystery; and the peridot, a deep yellowish green gem often associated with protection and enlightenment.

Again, it's important to note that the properties attributed to gems can differ considerably among authorities and traditions. Furthermore, the effects of gems seem to be a product of our interactions with them, which can vary widely among individuals.

SUMMARY

Even when compared with so-called precious or semiprecious gems, the quartz crystal remains one of nature's most important instruments of power. In fact, almost nothing seems beyond its powers. Aside from its commonly attributed capacity to receive, store, and send energy, it can be programmed with specific functions that can range from personal to global goals. All of these are within the scope of this amazing instrument of nature.

While a variety of empowerment attributes have been assigned to various gems by tradition and authorities, your best guide to the usefulness of gems is the nature of your personal interactions with them.

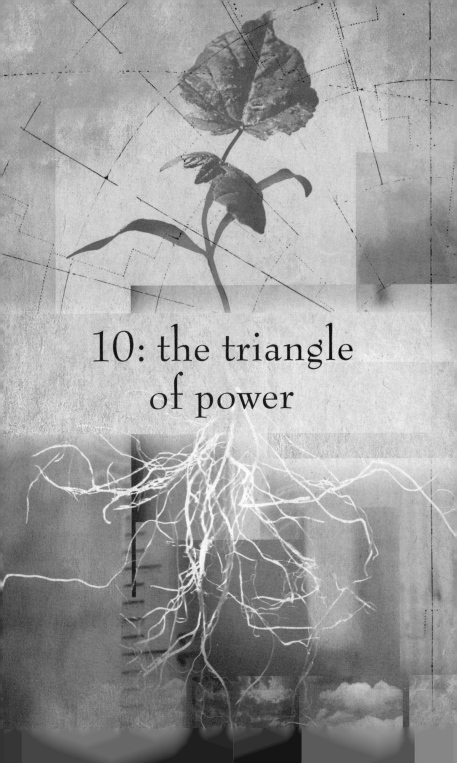

10: the triangle
of power

Learning is ever in the freshness of its youth, even for the old.
—AESCHYLUS

The greater your understanding of nature's empowering resources, the greater your understanding of yourself, and the more empowered you become to realize your highest destiny. The *Triangle of Power* is a step-by-step exercise specifically designed to facilitate that important growth process. The procedure is based on the simple premise that life force energy is without limits—it energizes our individual existence and the world around us while stretching to infinity to sustain all that exists, both seen and unseen. The technique uses a triangle formed by your hands as a frame for viewing nature and interacting with it. It's a practical exercise that becomes highly valued by almost everyone who uses it.

THE TRIANGLE OF POWER

The Triangle of Power has wide applications, and you can use it almost anywhere. It is easily adapted for indoor use when an outside scene is not available for viewing. Here's the procedure.

Step 1. Triangle Formation

To begin, clear your mind of active thought and then form a triangle with your hands by joining the tips of your thumbs for its base and the tips of your index fingers for its top. Think of the three sides of the triangle as representing the three components of your makeup: mind, body, and spirit. Think of the space within the triangle as representing the interactions of those three components and the totality of your existence—mentally, physically, and spirituality.

Step 2. Triangle Viewing

With your hands held at arm's length, use the triangle as a frame through which to view a nature scene or object, such as a tree, plant, lake, mountain, forest, or any combination of these. Other options include a cloud, the moon, or stars. Select a view that appeals to you personally, and adjust the frame by moving your hands in or out to find the ideal distance for viewing it. For indoor use, a potted plant can be substituted for viewing.

Step 3. Interaction

While viewing the selected scene or object through the triangle, sense your interaction with it. Let the life-force energies of nature flow into the triangle to merge with the life-force energies of your being. At this point, you may note a glow in the triangle as you sense the powerful merging of energies, first in your hands, and then throughout your total being—mentally, physically, and spiritually.

Step 4. Harmony, Balance, and Oneness
Once the merging of life force energies is complete, relax your hands, and with your eyes closed, turn your palms upward. Almost instantly, you will sense harmony and balance throughout your being, along with a complete oneness with the universe.

Step 5. Visualization and Enlightenment
As your eyes remain closed, visualize the triangle as a frame for enlightenment. Think of the triangle as a window for the merging of life force energy. Visualize a glow within the triangle as meaningful impressions and images spontaneously emerge. Allow plenty of time for enlightenment to unfold.

Step 6. Goal Statements and Empowerment Affirmation
State your personal goals one by one, and affirm your power to achieve them. Remind yourself that the power to meet any challenge, overcome any obstacle, and achieve any goal resides within your own being. Abundance, happiness, and success are now available to you.

Step 7. Conclusion
Conclude the procedure with the following affirmation: *I can at any time reactivate the full empowering effects of this*

experience by simply visualizing the triangle as a window for interacting with nature.

Central to the effectiveness of the Triangle of Power are your goal statement and related affirmations (Step 6). They become spiritual vibrations that reach to infinity once you're attuned to the life force energies within yourself and beyond. Abundance, happiness, and success are all within the scope of this powerful procedure.

The Triangle of Power provides a framework for your personal empowerment and success. Make your goals real in the triangle of power through imagery and affirmation, and they will become real in your life. Eventually you will achieve what you visualize and affirm. That doesn't mean you'll never encounter difficulties. Difficulties, you'll find, are simply exercises for growth—you become stronger by overcoming them.

Summary

The Triangle of Power is one of the most powerful ways known for interacting with nature and the universe at large. It unites the three major components of your existence— mind, body, and spirit. Through the resulting interaction, you'll discover new powers within yourself and beyond, along with new meaning to your life.

Through the Triangle of Power, you'll experience inner balance and attunement to the universe at large. You will become empowered to achieve your most difficult goals. The Triangle of Power manifests with certainty your destiny for greatness.

11: the seven–day discovery and empowerment plan

Let nature be your teacher.
—WILLIAM WORDSWORTH

You couldn't have chosen a better time to discover the empowering possibilities available to you through your interactions with nature. Now, as never before, you can experience them for yourself. Of all our growth resources, none is more accessible and worthy of trust than our natural surroundings. Because the empowering potential of nature has been tested and confirmed, it provides the standard against which other alternatives can now be judged.

Through the *Seven-day Discovery and Empowerment Plan* that follows, you can establish an unshakable foundation for your mental, physical, and spiritual evolvement. The plan is designed to jump-start a new growth process that will enrich and empower your life. Each day of the plan identifies an objective and presents a step-by-step program specifically designed to achieve it. Day by day, the plan provides the building blocks required to bring forth desired change, both within yourself and the world around you. Through the seven-day plan, you can take decisive action to achieve your highest goals while making the planet a better place for present and future generations.

As with other self-empowerment approaches, the seven-day plan presented here is a highly flexible program. Through repeated practice, you can increase the effectiveness of each daily program. Similarly, once the seven-day plan is complete, you can increase its overall effectiveness by again going through the full program.

In the final analysis, the all-encompassing purpose of our existence on this planet is to develop our highest potentials while contributing to the greater good. Through the plan that follows, you can take a major step toward achieving that important goal.

DAY ONE:
TREE LEAF EMPOWERMENT.

Day one is critical to our seven-day plan because it activates an upward growth spiral that sets the stage for the remaining six days. It introduces *Tree Leaf Empowerment* based on the twofold premise that (1) small things can make great beginnings and (2) great things are simply small things put together. Through a leaf taken from a tree of your choice, you can generate an energized mental, physical, and spiritual interaction with unlimited growth possibilities. Here's the program.

Step l. Select a Tree
Select a tree that appeals to you personally. Engage the tree by placing your hands upon its trunk while focusing on your goal of becoming mentally, physically, and spiritually empowered. Think of the tree as a powerful antennae and your link to the universe.

Step 2. Select a Leaf
Select a leaf that commands your attention, and before removing it from the tree, stroke it gently. Think of the leaf as a channel connecting you to the tree with its powerful reserve of energy.

Step 3. Engage the Leaf
Carefully remove the leaf from the tree and place it, topside up, in the palm of either hand. With the leaf resting in your hand, close your eyes and visualize a bright ray of energy connecting the leaf first to the tree from which it was

taken, and from there to infinity. Note the sense of serenity and well-being accompanying this step.

Step 4. Energy Infusion

Embrace the leaf by placing your other hand over it. With the leaf resting between your palms, think of it as your link to nature and the sustaining life force underlying it. Sense the powerful infusion of energy, first in your hands and then throughout your total being. Once the infusion of energy reaches its peak, return the leaf to the earth by placing it on the ground, preferably at the base of the tree from which it was taken.

Step 5. Conclusion

Having returned the leaf to the earth, stabilize the new infusion of energy using the so-called *Finger Interlock Technique* by bringing together the tips of the thumb and middle finger of each hand to form two circles, and then bringing your hands together to form interlocking circles. While holding the finger interlock position, visualize a bright glow of energy enveloping your full body as you affirm: *I am fully energized and empowered mentally, physically, and spiritually.*

You can use the Finger Interlock Technique at will as a cue throughout the seven-day plan and beyond to reactivate in an instant the full effects of the Tree Leaf Empowerment program. Aside from its instant energizing effect, you can use the cue to reduce stress and clear your mind. You can use it in the work setting to deal more effectively with people, increase your powers of concentration, and build your self-confidence. More specifically, you can use it—even with your hands behind your back—for such diverse goals as eliminating stage fright during public presentations or protecting yourself against any invading threat to your well-being. These are only a few of its many applications. With practice, you'll find this simple technique becomes even more powerful. Add it to your repertoire of skills and use it as needed to enrich the quality your life.

DAY TWO:
THE CLOUD OF POWER

Day two of our plan builds on the results of day one by introducing the *Cloud of Power*, specifically designed to generate new insight through interacting with higher planes of power. The step-by-step program uses a selected cloud, or if no cloud is available, an image of it, as a vehicle for enlightenment and growth. While not designed as an astral travel strategy, the program does generate a liberated state of ascended awareness during which interactions with spirit guides and teachers can occur. Here's the program.

Step 1. Relaxation
While in a comfortable, preferably reclining position in a safe outdoor setting, close your eyes, and take in a few deep breaths, exhaling slowly. Develop a slow, rhythmic breathing pattern as relaxation spreads throughout your body.

Step 2. Cloud Viewing
With your body relaxed and your mind cleared of active thought, view a selected cloud, noting such details as shape,

size, coloration, and position in the sky. (NOTE: If a cloud for viewing is unavailable, you can use visualization to create an imaginary cloud.)

Step 3. Cloud Connection

Close your eyes and visualize the cloud as you sense your connection to it. Think of the cloud as a source of energy and your link to the universe. Turn your palms upward and let the energies in your hands interact with the energies of the cloud and from there, the universe at large. You can facilitate that interaction by visualizing bright rays of light connecting your hands to the cloud.

Step 4. State of Oneness

As the infusion of energy continues, note your emerging sense of oneness with the universe. Allow plenty of time for the infusion of energy and accompanying state of oneness to reach their peaks.

Step 5. Ascended Awareness

At this important step, sense the freeing of restricted consciousness to result in a liberated state of ascended awareness. You can now experience other dimensions of reality and knowledge, including the spirit realm. As you remain in that ascended state, remind yourself that all you need to know is now available to you. Allow plenty of time for new knowledge and insight to unfold. Awareness of spirit helpers and guides often occurs at this important stage of the program.

Step 6. Conclusion

Once the state of ascended awareness has run its course, conclude the program by turning your attention to the quiet, innermost part of your being as you sense the continuous flow of bright new energy.

With mastery of this program, you have added a critical element to the seven-day plan. You have initiated not only a contact with nature's spiritual side but a oneness with it as well. You now have direct access to higher realms of enlightenment and power. The spirit realm with its ministering guides, helpers, and growth specialists is now available to bring abundance, happiness, and quality to your life.

DAY THREE:
THE SAND ENGAGEMENT PROGRAM

Day three of our plan introduces the *Sand Engagement Program* in which physical contact with a sample of sand becomes a source of balance and attunement within your innermost self and beyond. Any sample of dry sand can be used for this exercise that is similar in some ways to the Flowing Sand Program as discussed earlier in this book. Originally designed for outdoors use, the Sand Engagement Program can be used indoors with a tray of sand.

Step 1. Sensory Awareness

Take a handful of dry sand from the ground (or tray) and while holding it lightly in your cupped hands, notice its texture, weight, warmth, or coolness, and other characteristics.

Step 2. Earth Connection

Think of the sand in your hands as a miniature model of the planet. Sense the sand as your connection to the Earth it represents, and from there, to the universe.

Step 3. Earth Interaction

Slowly bring your hands closer together and lightly massage the sample of sand. Sense the sand in your hands as your link to the highest sources of power. Note your sense of balance and attunement with the universe as you continue to lightly massage the sample of sand.

Step 4. Release

Slowly release the sand and as it returns to the ground (or tray), sense again your connection to the earth and the universe at large. As the sand flows through your hands, notice the emergent sense of harmony and oneness with the universe.

Step 5. Conclusion

Conclude this program by bringing your palms together and affirming: *I am attuned and balanced mentally, physically, and spiritually. I am at harmony with the earth and the universe. I am endowed with the power required to achieve my highest goals and reach my highest destiny.*

Through this simple program, you can discover the satisfaction of interacting with the earth in a highly tangible way that brings new meaning into your life. The earth is a sacred orb in a great master plan, a physical habitat for our continued evolvement as soul beings. By being here, we've entrusted ourselves to the Earth; and equally as important, we've entrusted the earth to ourselves. For each of us, caring for the earth is not just another option—it's a fundamental responsibility. It must also be our unwavering commitment. Reaching our highest goals as evolving souls demands nurturing and protecting the Earth as a hallowed growth place for both present and future generations.

DAY FOUR:
THE PEBBLE IN A BOTTLE.

Day four of the plan introduces the *Pebble in a Bottle,* a program designed to unleash your inner powers, both conscious and subconscious, and target them on specific personal goal. This seven-step program uses water to represent your inner powers and pebbles to represent your stated goals. It's especially effective for such goals as breaking unwanted habits, overcoming persistent fears, solving pressing personal problems, building self-assurance, promoting better health and fitness, and even slowing the aging process. The program can also be used for goals of global relevance.

The only materials required for this program are a clear glass bottle (or jar) of water and a pebble for each of your stated goals. By dropping the pebble into the water with purpose, you can tap into your inner resources and focus them on the goal represented by the pebble.

Step 1. Goal Statement and Success Affirmation
To begin the program, formulate a specific personal goal and in your own words, affirm your potential to achieve it. The simple affirmation, *I will use my inner resources to*

achieve this important goal, effectively identifies the two critical elements of success: (1) a recognition of ability and (2) the expectation of success.

Step 2. Bottle Selection

Select a clear glass bottle (or jar) and fill it with clear water to represent your inner resources, both conscious and subconscious.

Step 3. Pebble Selection

Select a pebble to represent your stated goal. The pebble should be of a size that can rest comfortably in your hand and be dropped easily into the bottle of water.

Step 4. Pebble Interaction

While holding the pebble in your hand, sense its distinguishing characteristics such as weight, size, and texture. While stroking the pebble, remind yourself that it represents your stated goal and the water represents your potential to achieve it. Affirm that by dropping the pebble into the water, you will activate the inner resources required to achieve your goal.

Step 5. Empowerment Activation

Drop the pebble into the water and observe it as it sinks to the bottom. Once the pebble comes to rest, sense the activation of your inner powers, both conscious and subconscious, related to your stated goal.

Step 6. Success Affirmation

With the pebble at rest in the bottle, focus your attention on it as you affirm: *All the inner resources I need to achieve my goal of* (state goal) *are now activated. I will succeed!*

Step 7. Conclusion

Complete the program by placing the bottle where you can conveniently view it. You can reactivate the resources required to achieve your goal at any time by either viewing or visualizing the bottle with its water and pebble.

For multiple goals, you can use the same bottle of water, but with a different pebble for each goal. For each of your designated goals, select a pebble with features that you can readily associate with that goal if possible. For instance, if your goal is rejuvenation related, you may wish to select a symmetrical pebble with a smooth surface. If your goal is to develop your creative powers, you may prefer an irregularly shaped pebble with unusual features. For goals of global relevance, a spherical stone is recommended.

Barriers to your growth can function in at least two ways: (1) they can thwart your growth, or (2) they can challenge you to confront and overcome them. Fortunately, you can choose the function. By confronting and overcoming present barriers, you become stronger and better equipped to deal with future adversity and setbacks. By dropping a pebble into a bottle of water with purpose, you can choose success over defeat. You have all the resources you need to succeed. This simple program empowers you to activate them.

DAY FIVE:
THE SEED OF PROGRESS

The *Seed of Progress* is an other- rather than a self-oriented program. It's based on the simple premise that certain of our own growth potentials can be realized only by contributing to the greater good. For this six-step program, the greater good includes the well-being of others, both human and animal, as well as the globe. Though this program may seem lofty, it uses the simple seed of a plant or tree as a dynamic repository of potential that's receptive to our interaction.

Step 1. Goal Specification

Identify a goal related to the higher good and select a seed from a plant or tree to represent it. The goal could range from performing a simple daily act of kindness to becoming active in promoting a worthy cause of global relevance.

Step 2. Seed Connection

With the seed resting in your hand, note its unique characteristics. Think of it as a repository of great potential. Visualize the plant or tree from which the seed was taken, and think of the seed as representing its abundant energies. Think of the seed as your contact to the plant or tree, and the plant or tree as your contact to the universe. Stroke the seed as you sense its energies merging with your own.

Step 3. Seed Engagement

Bring your palms together, and with the seed between them, again state your goal as in Step 1. In your own words, engage the seed as your partner in achieving that goal.

Step 4. Visualization

With the seed resting between your hands, use visualization to give substance to your goal. For instance, if your goal is to bring happiness and abundance into another person's life, visualize that person enveloped in the bright energies of fulfillment. If your goal, on the other hand, is to promote global evolvement, envision the globe enveloped in the light of peace and progress. Notice vibrant energy, first in your hands and from there, surging throughout your body, a phenomenon that almost always accompanies visualization at this stage.

Step 5. Directed Action

As the seed continues to rest between your hands, affirm in your own words your unwavering commitment to your stated goal. Formulate a plan of action consistent with your goal. A modest act that contributes to the betterment of others can promote the higher good while enriching your own life.

Step 6. Conclusion

Either return the seed to the earth, preferably near the place from which it was taken, or keep it close at hand as a reminder of your goal and your commitment to achieve it.

Enrichment is the key word for day five of our plan. As evolving souls, we're here to grow and learn, while at the same time contributing to the betterment of others—persons and animals alike. Though it may seem simplistic, keep in mind that big things are made of small pieces put together. Small acts of kindness put together in sufficient quantity will have a global impact. Make acts of kindness a part of your personal discovery and empowerment plan, not just for today but for everyday of your life. You will benefit and so will the globe.

DAY SIX:
GLOBAL EVOLVEMENT PROGRAM

The plan for day six introduces the *Global Evolvement Program* designed specifically to promote the positive evolvement of the globe. The five-step program is based on the premise that global conditions are receptive to our intervention—they can in fact cry out to us to bring forth needed change in the world. Protecting human and animal rights, promoting world peace, and raising global consciousness may seem lofty, but they are all within the scope of this program.

Step 1. Centered Readiness

Begin the program by finding a quiet place, settling back, and letting your cares gently roll away. You can facilitate that process by centering your attention on the bright, inner space of serenity and peace.

Step 2. Universal Awareness

Expand awareness of your existence, not simply as a self-contained physical being, but as a spiritual entity without borders. Visualize the bright life force within yourself radiating outward and stretching to infinity. Affirm your interrelatedness to all that exists in the universe and beyond. Affirm your power not only to achieve your highest destiny, but to bring forth global change as well.

Step 3. Commitment to Global Progress

Identify an important goal related to global advancement, and affirm your commitment to contribute toward its fulfillment. Remind yourself that commitment to progress and change is the essential first step in raising global consciousness and solving global problems.

Step 4. Global Embracement

Having formulated your goals and affirmed your commitment to achieve them, embrace the globe by visualizing it enveloped in the bright light of renewal and progress. At this point, you can focus on global regions of concern, and mentally saturate them with light.

Step 5. Conclusion

Conclude the program by affirming your lasting commitment to global progress.

Commitment to global progress has never been more important than today. Our personal development (and empowerment) must include a concern for the globe, and a commitment to address global needs. Let's face it—the globe is at risk. Homelessness, suffering, hunger, social injustice, and reckless exploitation of natural resources—to list but a few—demand our attention and action now. Solving global problems is not an impossible dream—together, we can make it a reality.

DAY SEVEN:
THE MULTIPURPOSE
EMPOWERMENT PROGRAM

Taken together, the previous six days of our seven-day plan focused on providing the building blocks required to bring forth positive change and promote growth, both within ourselves and in the world around us. The goal of day seven is to provide the mortar that unites those building blocks into an integrated whole with a lasting synergistic effect.

This final day of our plan introduces the *Multipurpose Empowerment Program* that uses nature-related imagery to amplify and permanently sustain the seven-day plan's empowering effects. The result is an energized system and empowered state of mind, body, and spirit that simply cannot fail.

Step 1. Physical Relaxation

Settle back into a comfortable reclining position, and with your eyes closed, develop a rhythmic breathing pattern. Beginning at your forehead, let relaxation spread slowly down your body, soaking deep into your muscles and joints, right through the tips of your toes. Take plenty of time for every joint, muscle, fiber, and tendon to become fully relaxed.

Step 2. Power Imagery

With your body deeply relaxed, allow a series of peaceful images related to nature to flow gently through your mind. They could include, for instance, a moonlit cove, a colorful sunset, a lake with a sail in the distance, a mountain stream rippling over rocks, a forest trail winding among towering trees, a moonlit cove, or a fluffy cloud floating against the blue. Continue to focus on the flow of images until a particular image commands your special attention by lingering in your mind. Center your attention on that arrested image, noting in detail its characteristics. Sense your connection to the image as your contact to the abundant energies of the universe.

Step 3. Power Infusion

With the image lingering in your mind, turn your palms upward and sense the infusion of energy, first in your hands and from there throughout your total being—mentally, physically, and spiritually. Note the emerging sense of oneness with the universe that accompanies this simple gesture. Nothing is impossible for you in that empowered state.

Step 4. Temple Touch

Conclude by touching your temples with your fingertips to signify not only your oneness with the universe but your commitment to the higher good as well. You can use this simple gesture as a cue at will to reactivate the full effects of this program.

Now complete, the Seven-day Discovery and Empowerment Plan puts you in charge. You now have the power to achieve your highest goals and bring forth desired change in the world around you. You can now maximize your potential, improve the quality of your life, and make the world a better place.

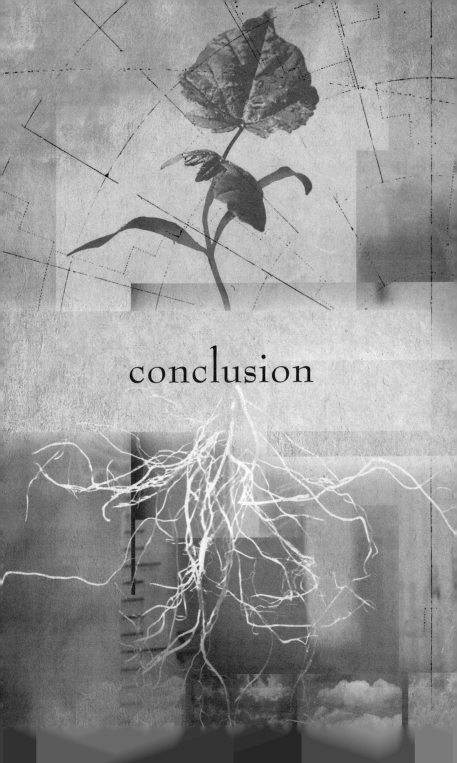

conclusion

From wonder into wonder existence opens.

—Lao-tzu

Through these pages, we've explored with wonderment the power of nature. Together, we've looked close-up and from a distance to experience the richness of nature's power. We've found inspiration and hope through the breathtaking beauty of our natural surroundings. We've experienced the abundant power of nature's tangible treasures, such as plants, soil, sand, and water. We've observed nature's noble creatures and learned from them. Through our exploration of nature, we've uncovered totally new sources of power, both within ourselves and beyond.

Although our interactions with nature provide many answers, they evoke the most challenging and searching question of all—*Who am I, and what is the meaning of my existence?* The answer to that must come only from you.

You've heard it before—as evolving souls, we're here to learn and grow while making the world a better place for present and future generations. Volumes have been written on that topic, but when you boil it down, it all comes to this:

1. **Knowledge.** Gain essential knowledge.
2. **Skills.** Acquire relevant skills.
3. **Application.** Apply the knowledge and skills.
4. **Persistence.** Once started, keep going.

Given knowledge, skills, application, and persistence, you can overcome any obstacle and achieve any goal. As a life-force being, nothing has power over you. You don't have to wait until tomorrow or the next world to have abundance, happiness, and success in your life—the possibilities are unlimited, and they are here and now.

It has been my lifelong philosophy that our destiny is twofold: endless growth and immeasurable greatness. I'm convinced that the best is yet to come, but with one critical caveat—we must each do what we can to make it happen. Knowledge is power, but power demands responsible action. It's time to seize the moment and create a new world of cooperation, fulfillment, and peace.

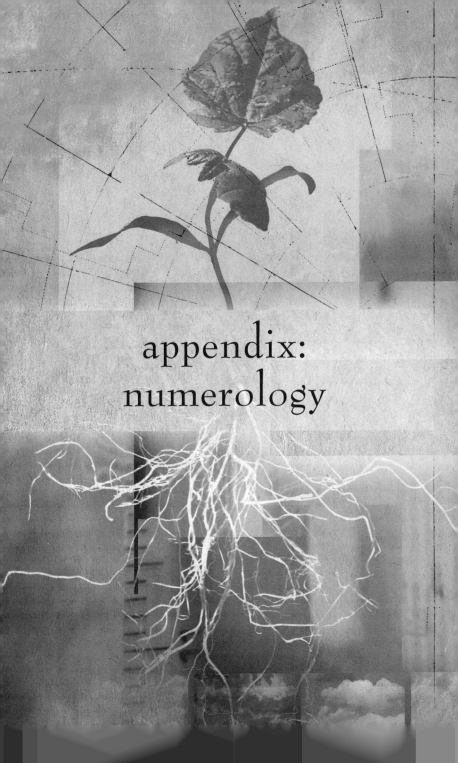

appendix:
numerology

In 550 BC, Pythagoras reduced the universal numerals to figures 1 through 9 and asserted that the world is built on the power of numbers. Around 2,000 years later, Cornelius Agrippa theorized that each number possessed significance beyond its numerical value. Consistent with that view, numerology today asserts each name as well as date has a vibratory number with certain signification.

The follow number/alphabet key can be used to determine name and date numbers by assigning a numerical value to each letter based on its place in the alphabet, and then summing the numerical values until they are reduced to a single digit:

A	B	C	D	E	F	G	H	I
J	K	L	M	N	O	P	Q	R
S	T	U	V	W	X	Y	Z	
1	2	3	4	5	6	7	8	9

Using this key, the letters A, J, and S have a numerical value of 1; whereas letters B, K, and T have a numerical value of 2 and so forth. To determine the numerical value of a name, including your own, simply add the numerical values of all letters in the name until the sum is reduced to a single digit. For example, the single digit value for the name Robert Jones is computed as follows:

R O B E R T   J O N E S
9+6+2+5+9+2+1+6+5+5+1 = 51 = 6.

Using this key, Robert Jones has a name number of 6.

While it must be noted that the significance of name numbers vary considerably among sources, the commonly assigned numerological values are as follows:

Number 1: Independence and self-reliance.

Number 2: Antithesis and balance.

Number 3: Versatility and talent.

Number 4: Steadiness and solidity.

Number 5: Bold and adventurous.

Number 6: Dependable and trustworthy person.

Number 7: Mystery and knowledge.

Number 8: Achievement and authority.

Number 9: Self-realization and personal empowerment.

Based on these values, Robert Jones with a name number of 6 is a dependable person.

To determine the numerical value of a date (including one's birth date), the position of each month in the year is usually added to the numbers found in the day and year. For instance, the date 7/11/2006 has a numerological value of 8, which signifies achievement and authority. An alternate approach determines the numerical value for the name of the month and then adds that value to the day and year.

suggested
reading

Bartholomew, M. *Square Foot Gardening*. Emmaus, PA: Rodale Press, 1981.

Berry, T. *The Dream of the Earth.* San Francisco: Sierra Club Books, 1988.

Buell, L. *The Environmental Imagination: Thoreau, Nature Writing, and the Formation of American Culture.* Cambridge, MA: Harvard University Press, 1995.

Chard, P. *The Healing Earth: Nature's Medicine for the Troubled Soul.* Minocqua, WI: NorthWord, 1994.

Conner, M. "Wilderness therapy programs: a powerful intervention for adolescents." *The National Psychologist,* Vol. 16, No. 11, 14–15, 2007.

Garland, H. *Main Traveled Roads.* New York: Signet, 1962.

Guiness, B. *Creating a Family Garden: Magical Outdoor Spaces for All Ages.* New York: Abbeville Press, 1996.

James, M., and D. Jongward. *Born to Win.* Reading, MA: Addison-Wesley, 1971.

Levine, M. *Wonder of Life.* New York: Golden Press, 1968.

Louv, Richard. *Last Child in the Woods.* New York: Algonquin, 2006.

Metzner, R. *Spirit, Self, and Nature: Essays in Green Psychology.* El Veno, CA: Green Earth, 1993.

Miller, W., ed. *Integrating Spirituality into Treatment.* Washington, DC: American Psychological Assn., 1999.

Miller, W., and H. Delaney, eds. *Judeo-Christian Perspectives on Psychology.* Washington, DC: American Psychological Assn., 2005.

Osborn, A. *Your Creative Power.* New York: Scribners, 1949.

Richards, P., and A. E. Bergin. *A Spiritual Strategy for Counseling and Psychotherapy* (2nd ed.). Washington, DC: American Psychological Assn., 2005.

Richards, P., and A. Bergin, eds. *Casebook for a Spiritual Strategy in Counseling and Psychotherapy.* Washington, DC: American Psychological Assn., 2004.

———. *Handbook of Psychotherapy and Religious Diversity.* Washington, DC: American Psychological Assn., 2000.

Richards, P., R. Hardman, and M. Berrett. *Spiritual Approaches in the Treatment of Women with Eating Disorders.* Washington, DC: American Psychological Assn., 2007.

Roberts, C. *Eyes of the Wilderness.* New York: Macmillan, 1936.

———. *The Kindred of the Wild.* New York: Blue Ribbon Books, 1937.

Roszak, T. *The Voice of the Earth: An Exploration in Ecopsychology.* New York: Simon & Schuster, 1992.

Sagan, Carl. *The Cosmic Connection.* New York: Dell, 1973.

Saltz, G. *Becoming Real: Defeating the Stories We Tell Ourselves That Hold Us Back.* New York: Penguin, 2005.

Sills, J. *The Comfort Trap or What If You're Riding a Dead Horse.* New York: Penguin, 2005.

Slate, Joe H. *Aura Energy for Health, Healing, & Balance.* Woodbury, MN: Llewellyn, 1999.

———. *Beyond Reincarnation.* Woodbury, MN: Llewellyn, 2005.

———. *Psychic Empowerment: A 7-day Plan for Self-development.* Woodbury, MN: Llewellyn, 1995.

———. *Psychic Empowerment for Health and Fitness.* Woodbury, MN: Llewellyn, 1996.

———. *Psychic Phenomena: New Principles, Techniques and Applications.* Jefferson, NC: McFarland, 1988.

———. *Rejuvenation: Living Younger, Longer & Better.* Woodbury, MN: Llewellyn, 2001.

———. *Self Empowerment: Strategies for Success.* Bessemer, AL: Colonial Press, 1991.

Tippett, J. *Paths to Conservation.* New York: Heath, 1937.

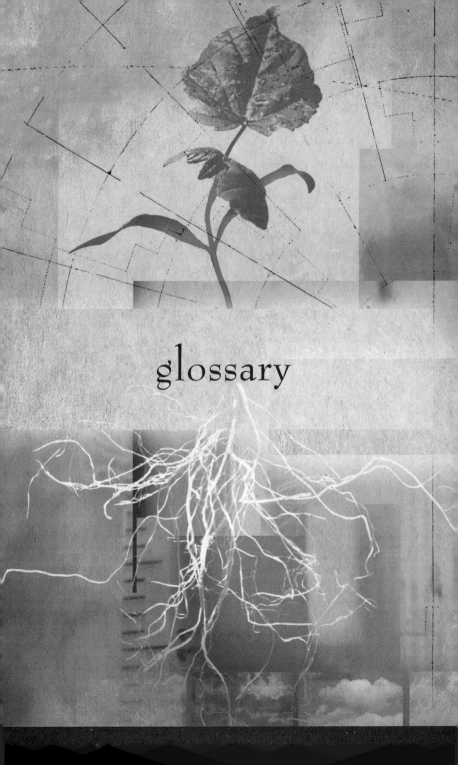

glossary

agritherapy. A psychotherapy approach based on the therapeutic value of working in soil and nurturing plants.

aura. A colorful energy phenomenon enveloping the physical body and believed to be an external manifestation of
an inner energy core.

aura massage. An energy interaction in which the energies
enveloping the physical body are massaged in the absence
of physical touch.

automatic sand writing. A technique in which spontaneous,
effortless writing on the smooth surface of sand becomes
a source of relevant information or creative expression.

automatic writing. A technique designed to access subconscious sources of information through effortless, spontaneous writing.

Bottomless Pool Ritual. A practice of tossing a ring or other
object representing a relationship into a certain pool—
believed by some to be bottomless—as a gesture to fully
disengage a no longer viable relationship and extinguish
its residual effects. See *Disengagement Toss Procedure.*

Center of Power. A ritual that consists of placing seed from
a plant or tree in a geometric arrangement on the ground

or other flat surface and meditating at its center to connect oneself to distant energy sources, including the parent plant or tree from which the seeds were taken.

clinical sand reading. A projective technique in which the subject describes the characteristics seen in the hand imprint in sand.

Cloud of Power. A program designed to extend awareness and facilitate interactions with higher planes of power through use of a selected cloud, or image of it.

Crumpled Leaf. An exercise based on the capacity of a leaf to function as an instrument of power when removed from the tree.

crystal clearing. A program designed to clear the quartz crystal of all previous inscriptions or residual effects.

crystal programming. A program designed to establish an empowering interaction with a quartz crystal in an effort to focus the crystal's energies or influences on designated goals.

Disengagement Toss. A ritual designed to facilitate disengagement in a non-viable relationship and promote resolution of its residual effects by tossing a ring or other article of jewelry representing the relationship into a body of water. See *Bottomless Pool Ritual.*

distance healing. The transfer of healing influences or energies from a spatial distance.

distance intervention. The intervention of a power source from a spatial distance.

Flowing Sand. A program based on the empowering effects of a handful of sand flowing through the fingers.

forest therapy. A therapeutic approach that recognizes the forest as a therapist.

Garden Empowerment. A program designed to facilitate empowering interactions with plants in a garden setting.

Global Evolvement. A program designed to promote the evolvement of the globe.

interactive effect. The resultant increase in effectiveness when two or more exercises or resources are combined.

Multipurpose Empowerment. A program that uses nature-related imagery to uncover new sources of power, both within oneself and beyond.

Nature Walk. A program designed to promote a positive interaction with nature, typically by walking in a forest and focusing the forest's energies on designated goals.

NDE. See *near-death experience.*

near-death experience (NDE). An experience in which one's death appears imminent, often accompanied by a sense of separation of consciousness from the biological body.

numerology. The study of numbers and their significance beyond the expression of quantity.

Pebble in a Bottle. A program using a pebble and bottle of water to access the subconscious and unleash its hidden or dormant powers.

Pebble and Pail. An adaptation of the Pebble and Pool program in which a pail of water is used as a substitute for a pool. See *Pebble and Pond.*

Pebble and Pond. A goal-directed program in which a pebble dropped into a pool is used to deepen one's resolve to achieve designated goals.

Pebble of Commitment and Vessel of Faith. A program in which a pebble is dropped into a vessel of water as a symbolic representation of commitment and faith, particularly in goals related to spiritual efforts.

phantom leaf effect. In electrophotography, a phenomenon in which the energy pattern enveloping a full leaf remains intact after a part of the leaf is removed.

Plant Interaction. A program using a selected plant to represent a goal and ensure success in achieving it.

sand reading. A technique in which a hand imprint made in a tray of sand provides a point of focus and possible source of new information.

Seed of Success. A ritual using the seeds of plants to facilitate achievement of long range goals, such as career success, financial security, better health and fitness, longevity, and self-development.

Soil Engagement. A goal-related program in which physical contact with a sample of soil becomes a source of motivation and power.

Star Gaze. A program that selects a star or group of stars as a point of focus to connect oneself to the life force within and beyond.

Stream of Success. An exercise utilizing imagery of a stream of water to promote physical relaxation and a positive state of mind.

Tree Leaf Empowerment. A program designed to generate a revitalized mental, physical, and spiritual state through interaction with a leaf and the tree from which it was taken.

Tree Power. A program designed to facilitate an empowering interaction with a tree as an instrument of nature.

Triangle of Power. A technique in which a triangle formed by the hands is used as a frame for viewing and interacting with the spiritual side of nature.

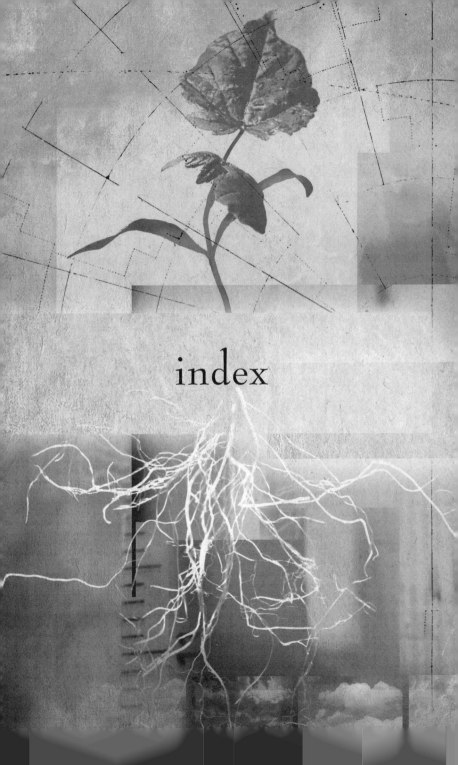

index

 **Free Catalog**

☾ LLEWELLYN ORDERING INFORMATION

Order Online:
Visit our website at www.llewellyn.com, select your books, and order them on our secure server.

Order by Phone:
- Call toll-free within the U.S. at 1-877-NEW-WRLD (1-877-639-9753). Call toll-free within Canada at 1-866-NEW-WRLD (1-866-639-9753)
- We accept VISA, MasterCard, and American Express

Order by Mail:
Send the full price of your order (MN residents add 6.875% sales tax) in U.S. funds, plus postage & handling to:

> **Llewellyn Worldwide**
> **2143 Wooddale Drive, Dept. 978-0-7387-1566-7**
> **Woodbury, MN 55125-2989**

Postage & Handling:

Standard (U.S., Mexico & Canada). If your order is:
$24.99 and under, add $4.00
$25.00 and over, FREE STANDARD SHIPPING

AK, HI, PR: $16.00 for one book plus $2.00 for each additional book.

International Orders (airmail only):
$16.00 for one book plus $3.00 for each additional book

Orders are processed within 2 business days.
Please allow for normal shipping time. Postage and handling rates subject to change.

Flower and Tree Magic
Discover the Natural Enchantment Around You

RICHARD WEBSTER

Did you know that flowers have a unique language of their own? Or that the way you draw a tree reflects your life outlook and personality?

Flowers and trees have long been celebrated as sacred and powerful. By learning to read the special messages they hold, plants can help us navigate our life path and reconnect with nature. In this comprehensive guide, bestselling author Richard Webster uncovers the hidden properties of every major type of tree, herb, and flower that we encounter in our daily lives. From protection and healing to divination and worship, this book shows you how to apply ancient spiritual practices from many cultures to modern life—attract your ideal mate with valerian and sage, ward off psychic attacks with a sprinkling of rose oil, restore positive energy with nature meditations, and more.

Nature lovers, myth historians, and trivia lovers alike will embrace this all-encompassing guide to the vast history and extensive magic of flowers and trees.

978-0-7387-1349-6, 240 pp., 6 x 9 $15.95

Feng Shui in the Garden
RICHARD WEBSTER

Whether you own an estate with formal gardens or live in a studio apartment with room for a few flowerpots, you can discover the remarkable benefits of using plants to create more ch'i (universal energy) in your life. Wherever you find an abundance of ch'i, the vegetation looks rich and healthy, the air smells fresh and sweet, and the water is cool and refreshing.

The ancient Chinese believed that when you live in harmony with the earth, you become a magnet for health, wealth, and happiness. *Feng Shui in the Garden* shows beginning and expert gardeners alike how to tailor their gardens to bring them the greatest amount possible of positive energy. Select your most beneficial location, layout, flowers, colors, fragrances, herbs, and garden accessories based on proven feng shui principles. Discover the optimum placement of fountains, waterfalls, or swimming pools. Learn how to construct a serene secret garden, even if you live in an apartment!

978-1-56718-793-9, 192 pp., 5¼ x 8 $9.95

Energy for Life
Connect with the Source
COLLEEN DEATSMAN

Lightning. Water. Sunshine. Apples. All matter is composed of energy, even ourselves. So what happens when our energy dissipates, becomes stagnant, or blocked? Imbalanced energy can jeopardize our quality of life and health—leading to fatigue, depression, or chronic illness. Colleen Deatsman's proven program for energy harmony demonstrates how to reignite and fortify one's vital life force energy.

This guide to energy work is full of easy energizing techniques to clear blockages, seal energy leaks, access universal life energy, and strengthen your energy field. Guided journeys, meditations, and other exercises can help you relax, de-stress, boost your energy, improve flow, and connect with spirit guides and other divine energies. *Energy for Life* also includes a handy audio CD of guided meditations.

978-0-7387-0774-7, 216 pp., 6 x 9 $19.95

To order, call 1-877-NEW-WRLD
Prices subject to change without notice
Order at Llewellyn.com 24 hours a day, 7 days a week!

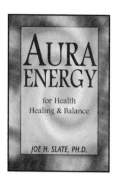

Aura Energy for Health, Healing & Balance
Joe H. Slate, Ph.D.

Imagine an advanced energy/information system that contains the chronicle of your life—past, present, and future. By referring to it, you could discover exciting new dimensions to your existence. You could uncover important resources for new insights, growth, and power.

You possess such a system right now. It is your personal aura. In his latest book, Dr. Joe H. Slate illustrates how each one of us has the power to see the aura, interpret it, and fine-tune it to promote mental, physical, and spiritual well-being. College students have used his techniques to raise their grade-point averages, gain admission to graduate programs, and eventually get the jobs they want. Now you can use his aura empowerment program to initiate an exciting new spiral of growth in all areas of your life.

978-1-56718-637-6, 264 pp., 6 x 9 $14.95

Essential Herbal Wisdom
A Complete Exploration of 50 Remarkable Herbs
Nancy Arrowsmith

Popular author and healing practitioner Nancy Arrowsmith takes readers on a fascinating, in-depth exploration of herbs in *Essential Herbal Wisdom*. Arrowsmith's friendly voice and vast knowledge of herbal applications, history, and folklore shine through in this holistic reference work. As entertaining as it is practical, this comprehensive illustrated guide covers everything from herb gathering prayers and charms to detailed herbal correspondences for fifty powerful herbs.

Each individual herb is described in detail, with tips on growing, gathering, drying, and storing, as well as on the herb's culinary virtues, cosmetic properties, medicinal merits, veterinary values, and household applications. Along with thought-provoking bits of folk history, and literary and spiritual references to herbs and nature, this directory includes step-by-step instructions on herbal dyeing, strewing, garlanding, and festooning, as well as gardening hints and seed-saving tips.

978-0-7387-1488-2, 576 pp., 7 x 10 $29.95